Grace to Help in Time of Need

A Collection of Sermons

David Johnson

This is a collection of sermons preached at Christ Episcopal Church in Valdosta, Georgia, by the Rev. Dr. David Johnson. The sermons do not now, nor have ever had any connection, affiliation, or sponsorship with any of the author(s), artists(s), or publications quoted or referenced herein. The content is intended for the purpose of commentary, study, discussion, literary and religious critique.

GRACE TO HELP IN TIME OF NEED

All rights reserved.

Published by David Johnson

Copyright © 2019 by David Johnson

This book is protected under the copyright laws of the United States of America. Any reproduction or other unauthorized use of the material or artwork herein is prohibited without the express written permission of the author.

Unless otherwise indicated, all scripture citations are from *The New Revised Standard Version Bible*.

References to *The Book of Common Prayer* are indicated as *BCP*.

Printed in the United States of America

First Edition

ISBN-9781702386029

Dedicated to those who feel helpless, who need God to be "a very present help in trouble" (Psalm 46:1).

Acknowledgments

Thanks to Christ Episcopal Church in Valdosta, Georgia—and for the privilege of receiving God's grace with you every week and sharing that grace with one another and the world. Thanks to the brilliant and hilarious John Zahl for his inspiring friendship and for writing the preface. Thanks to CJ Green for his outstanding editorial work. Thanks to Julius Ariail for the cover photograph, and to Bill Shenton for the cover design. Thanks to my family, my favorite people on the planet. Most of all, thanks to God for giving me "grace to help in time of need," too many times to count.

Contents

Preface: *From the Reverend John A. Zahl*	11
Introduction	15
Against All Odds (John 15:12-17)	17
You Have Eternal Life (1 John 5:11-13)	25
Where Your Strength Ends, God's Grace Begins (Romans 8:26-27)	33
The Lord of the Sabbath (Mark 2:23-28)	41
The Tender Love of Your Heavenly Father (2 Corinthians 5:14-17)	49
The Sure Foundation of God's Lovingkindness (Mark 4:35-41)	57
Your Eternal Superlative (Ephesians 1:3-6)	65
Jesus, Your Compassionate Shepherd (Mark 6:30-34)	73
Psalms and Hymns and Spiritual Songs (Ephesians 5:18-19)	81

Good News for the Brokenhearted (Psalm 34:18-20)	89
The Gospel is not a Grand Illusion (Mark 7:32-35)	95
The Inescapable Question (Mark 8:27-30)	103
The Powerful Mercy of God (Mark 9:42-48)	111
Grace? Grace. (Hebrews 10:14-18)	119
Your Redemption is Drawing Near (Luke 21:25-28)	127
Grace for Those Drifting too Far from the Shore (Luke 3:1-6)	135
Good News in an Age of Anxiety (Philippians 4:6-7)	143
God Lifts Up the Lowly (Luke 1:52)	151
The Rising of the Grace of God: A Christmas Sermon (Luke 2:8-16)	159
Grace and Truth Came through Jesus Christ (John 1:17)	167
Jesus Saves the Best for Last (John 2:1-11)	175
Very Real Spiritual Hope (Luke 4:16-21)	183
In Fact Christ Has Been Raised from the Dead (1 Corinthians 15:12-20)	191
No Myth at All (2 Corinthians 3:17)	199
New and Contrite Hearts: Ash Wednesday (Psalm 51:11)	207
Grace in the Wilderness of Temptation (Luke 4:1-13)	213
The Lord Helps Those Who Cannot Help Themselves (Exodus 3:1-15)	221

Totally Unbelievable and Yet Completely True (Luke 15:11-24)	229
Defined by the Grace of God (Philippians 3:4-14)	237
The Faithful Love of Your Humble God: Palm Sunday (Philippians 2:5-11)	245
Jesus Was Rejected for You: Good Friday (Isaiah 53:3)	251
All Will Be Made Alive in Christ: Easter Sunday (1 Corinthians 15:19-22)	257

Preface

The world we live in constantly tells us to "do more" and "try harder." We are told that "it is up to you/us to solve [y]our problems." It is precisely into this setting that the preached word of divine grace finds a fresh foothold. The Gospel stands out in high relief against a backdrop of messages from the culture having to do with romantic notions of personal mastery. Dave Johnson understands this as well as any contemporary preacher.

With Dave in the pulpit, one always receives a word of comfort and compassion. It's no wonder that the church he serves, Christ Church, Valdosta, is flourishing by every metric. And how fortunate we are to receive this volume of sermons from his ministry.

But in a day and age marked primarily by mainline denominational decline, there are reasons for this one church's growth. Dave has not invented a (new) wheel; he has simply bedded down in a methodology that is rarely found anymore in the Episcopal Church. Allow me to draw attention to a few of the main animating building blocks.

First and foremost, Dave preaches grace. He preaches Grace, as opposed to the Law. His sermons are not designed to tell you what to do. Instead, they tell you about the One who "has done all things well," and who has done so for your and my sake. It's a

24/7/365 approach to ministry: grace is the main chestnut. Just as you will hear words of grace every Sunday from the Christ Church pulpit, so too you will experience them in Dave's pastoral care whether in his office or prayerfully from the confines of a hospital bed when he comes to visit you; you'll experience them on the back of T-shirts at Christ Church's Grace Café where "it's not cheap; it's free." ...and if you have ever texted with Dave Johnson before, then you know that even his texts are like little grace cherry bombs, exuding love and "no pressure" *ad infinitum*.

Furthermore, this book underscores the centrality of preaching in the life of Dave's parish. This is not because the author of these sermons likes the sound of his own voice. No, the reason for the emphasis has to do with the fact that the main reason most people are drawn to visit a church on a Sunday morning is because they are hoping that the sermon will speak to them (i.e., about their real lives). They are looking for a word of hope that reorients their perspective and enables them to face the coming week with fresh confidence. Ultimately, it is a word that connects the listener in a fresh way to God, and God to the listener.

In church, whether we like it or not, the sermon is the actual focal point. It determines the tone of everything else we do together on Sunday morning. And, unfortunately, most sermons are either abstract, or they are law-driven. Either they don't engage the person in the pew at a gut level, or they only engage the person in the pew practically by adding to that person's already burdensome to-do list. It's no wonder so many Episcopal churches think that the Eucharist is the central act of worship. For, in many cases, that's the only place in church where the faithful are being given anything of grace that they can personally digest.

But the problem is that, for better or for worse, the Eucharist does not initially speak to the newcomer as clearly as a sermon containing the same content. First and foremost, it is the sermon that is capable of creating within the hearts of its hearers a "conversion." The Eucharist, in turn, is a vehicle for *sustaining* that which was first created through the preaching. In practice, it is preaching that creates, and the Eucharist that sustains. And, when aligned, the two complement each other brilliantly. As Thomas Cranmer put it, "For as the word of God preached putteth Christ into our ears; so likewise these elements of water, bread, and wine, joined to God's word, do, after a sacramental manner, put Christi into our eyes, mouths, hands, and all our senses." Notice that, for the one who first created *The Book of Common Prayer*, it was the preached word that enlivened the experience of the sacraments, and has in and of itself "a sacramental manner."

And Dave Johnson does not just preach a particular piece of Christian doctrine (e.g., "Jesus Christ died to save sinners"), for there is a difference between good doctrine and a good sermon. You see, Dave Johnson preaches a particular message of grace (a.k.a., the Gospel) *well*. Preaching well in his case brings with it three elements.

The first is his inimitable use of pop culture. Dave sees the dynamics of grace playing out in the world all around him. He points out, for example, themes of grace in the lyrics of John Lennon, Bob Dylan, and Journey; in movies like *Jaws* and *The Godfather, Part 2*; and even in popular television shows like *Parks & Recreation*. The same goes for sporting references. It's a style that is simultaneously down-to-earth, creative, and winsome. You can almost hear his parishioners on the drive home from church: "I can't believe he mentioned Belinda Carlisle!"

The second piece builds from the first, and that is Dave's incredible use of illustration. This is where he breathes life into the ideas and escapes from the pitfalls of platitude-laden preaching. Stories and imagery circumvent the head, and enable the listener to find a bridge between the ideas being proclaimed, and the hearts where those ideas can take root. Dave takes his cue from his Lord, who famously did the same thing using parables. This collection of sermons is a lesson (and resource) to any preacher looking to appreciate how to use illustrations to drive home one's intended point.

Finally, and most importantly, Dave is primarily interested in addressing one particular part of the human psyche: the part of the person who is suffering. He does this so effectively, because he knows what life is actually like. The understanding is that the church is "a hospital for sinners," and not a museum of saints. The target is always: the problematic portion of the hearer's life (which, if truth be told, is where most of our thoughts are centered most of the time). He knows all too well the truth of what another famous preacher, Sam Shoemaker, stated: "Everyone either has a problem, is a problem, or lives with a problem." Into this existential miasma, Dave unleashes the ameliorating word of grace, like a heat-seeking missile, and he does so with the assumption that the balm of Gilead, which is the love of God in Christ, is needed by almost everyone in the pews in some way every single week. It's a one-size-fits all message, and it never grows tiresome. Like I said at the outset: 24/7/365.

In short, *Grace to Help in Time of Need* is filled to the brim with "comfortable words" for those who "travail and are heavy laden." They spill forth from every page. He points the bound and burdened to the great burden-carrier, who is Jesus, the friend of sinners and the one who "has *grace to help in time of need*" (Hebrews 4:16).

John Zahl+ (Oct. 23, 2019)
Rector, St. Matthew's Episcopal Church
Bedford, New York

Introduction

This book is a collection of sermons I preached at Christ Episcopal Church in Valdosta, Georgia. The title of this book, *Grace to Help in Time of Need*, comes from one of the most moving passages from the Letter to the Hebrews:

> Since, then, we have a great high priest who has passed through the heavens, Jesus, the Son of God, let us hold fast to our confession. For we do not have a high priest who is unable to sympathize with our weaknesses, but we have one who in every respect has been tested as we are, yet without sin. Let us therefore approach the throne of grace with boldness, so that we may receive mercy and find *grace to help in time of need* (Hebrews 4:14-16, italics mine).

In every one of our lives, there are circumstances in which we are unable to help ourselves, circumstances that defy our efforts to "take care of it," circumstances in which "human help is worthless" (Psalm 60:11), circumstances in which we have no choice but to look to God for help. And the good news of the gospel is that when we do that, God indeed helps us with grace, unconditional love that never changes no matter what those circumstances may be. As the late preacher and author Brennan Manning used to say, "God loves you as you are, not as you should be, because no one is as they should be." When we are unable to help ourselves, God offers "grace to help in time of need." This is a recurring theme in the Book of Psalms, where we are reminded that God is "our help and shield" (33:20), our "help and deliverer" (40:17), "a very present help in trouble" (46:1)—in short, that "Our help is in the name of the Lord, who made heaven and earth" (124:8). In the most vulnerable of the letters of the Apostle Paul, his Second Letter to the Corinthians, he writes about a circumstance in which he was unable to help himself and in which human help was worthless, a "thorn in the flesh" that he refused to specify. When he asked, begged actually, the Lord to remove this circumstance, the Lord assured him, "My grace is sufficient for you, for power is made perfect in weakness" (12:9). What is true for the psalmists and the Apostle Paul is true for you. So whatever circumstances you currently face in which you need help from God, may this book be a source of encouragement and comfort, and may God abundantly give you "grace to help in time of need."

Against All Odds

This is my commandment, that you love one another as I have loved you. No one has greater love than this, to lay down one's life for one's friends. You are my friends if you do what I command you. I do not call you servants any longer, because the servant does not know what the master is doing; but I have called you friends, because I have made known to you everything that I have heard from my Father. You did not choose me but I chose you. And I appointed you to go and bear fruit, fruit that will last, so that the Father will give you whatever you ask him in my name. I am giving you these commands so that you may love one another (John 15:12-17).

In the Name of the Father, Son, and Holy Spirit.

Recently *National Geographic* published an article about an avid outdoor enthusiast named Dylan McWilliams, who has paid the price multiple times for his outdoor adventures. Earlier this year Dylan was attacked by a tiger shark while surfing in Hawaii. Last year while he was on a camping trip in Colorado he was bitten on the head by a black bear, and in 2015 while hiking in Utah he was stung by a rattlesnake. Poor Dylan McWilliams!

Now statistically the odds of being attacked by a shark in U. S. waters are 11.5 million to one, the odds of being bitten by a bear in the U.S. are 2.1 million to one, and the odds of being stung by a venomous snake are 37,500 to one. All this means that the odds of one person, like the apparently unlucky Dylan McWilliams suffering all three of these is an astonishing 893.35 quadrillion to one…and yet, against all conceivable odds, it happened (Stephen Leahy, April 24, 2018).

When we talk about the gospel, about the odds of a holy, omnipresent, omnipotent, omniscient God loving neurotic sinners like us, the odds would be even larger than 893.35 quadrillion to one…and yet it happened historically and definitively in Jesus' death on the cross, an act of love that defies all odds for all time.

In today's gospel passage from John's account of the Last Supper, Jesus talked about the most important thing in the world, love—loving one another with the same love Jesus would demonstrate the next day on Calvary:

> This is my commandment, that you love one another as I have loved you. No one has greater love than this, to lay down one's life for one's friends. You are my friends if you do what I command you. I do not call you servants any longer, because the servant does not know what the master is doing; but I have called you friends, because I have made known to you everything that I have heard from my Father. You did not choose me but I chose you (John 15:12-16).

Jesus assured his disciples that even though they had not chosen him, he had chosen them, as John later wrote in his First Letter: "In this is love, not that we loved God but that he loved us and sent his Son to be the atoning sacrifice for our sins…We love because God first loved us" (1 John 4:10, 19).

You may have heard it said one way or another that your life is the sum total of the choices you make, or as the nineteenth century philosopher and poet Ralph Waldo Emerson put it, "Sow a thought and you reap an action; sow an action and you reap a habit; sow a habit and you reap a character; sow a character and you reap a destiny." When it comes to your earthly life, you may have experienced the truth in that, the truth of what the Old Testament prophet Hosea wrote, "Sow the wind…reap the whirlwind" (Hosea 8:7).

And yes, your choices matter. You know that. In the Old Testament, Joshua, after leading Israel into the Promised Land, famously exhorted Israel to make the right choice: "Choose this day whom you will serve, whether the gods that your ancestors served in the region beyond the River or the gods of the Amorites in whose land you are living; but as for me and my household, we will serve the Lord" (Joshua 24:15). "Choose this day whom you will serve"…that is the law.

But again, as Jesus assured his disciples at the Last Supper, "You did not choose me but I chose you"…that is the gospel. Because the truth is that more often than not we do not make the right choices; as the Apostle Paul put it, "I can will what is right, but I cannot do it. For I do not do the good I want, but the evil I do not want is what I do" (Romans 7:18-19). Can you relate to that? If you do not relate to it now, trust me, someday you will. Our choices fall short, and that is where the good news of the gospel meets us. "You did not choose me, but I chose you." That is the gospel. Against all odds, Jesus has chosen you.

A couple illustrations—one from Hollywood, and a second from the NFL draft… I am sucker for romantic comedies. As you know, all romantic comedies tell the basic same story: amidst hilarious hijinks a couple meets and falls in love. Then they break up, only to be reunited against all odds at the end of the film. One of my favorite romantic comedies is the 1998 hit *The Wedding Singer* starring Adam Sandler as a down-on-his-luck wedding singer named Robbie Hart who falls madly in love with a beautiful waitress named Julia Sullivan, played by Drew Barrymore.

In the midst of this goofy romantic comedy, there is a powerful scene of grace. Robbie is singing at a bar mitzvah and notices one of the teenage guys looking very depressed. He walks over to him: "You seem kind of sad. Why don't you go over there and dance, buddy?" "I asked that girl over there," the sad boy replies; "she turned me down. She said she doesn't dance with losers." Robbie continues, "Oh man. That hurts. But, you know, why would you want to dance with somebody who doesn't want to dance with you, right? Listen, don't worry. You're gonna meet a girl who treats you right someday, I promise you."

Then Robbie returns to the mic and says to the crowd, "I'd like you to meet a friend of mine by the name of Julia Sullivan." He beckons her to the stage and continues, "Say hi to Julia everybody. Now who of you out there would like to dance with this fine-looking woman?" All the guys are raising their hands, and some are jumping up and down. "Wow, Julia," Robbie says; "sounds to me like you got your pick of any man in this room to dance with, so I want you to take your time and find amongst all these young studs here tonight the coolest, most un-loser-y guy in the bunch."

As Julia walks down the line, each of the boys tries to persuade her to pick him as they flex their muscles or smile seductively or show off their expensive clothes—"Please pick me! Please, Julia!" But to the shock of everyone, Julia stops in front of the goofiest, pudgiest kid there, the sad boy to whom Robbie had earlier spoken, who is sitting down and not paying any attention because he is used to never being chosen for anything, ever. Julia bends down toward him, smiles, takes his hand, and asks, "May I have this dance?" The boy is completely stunned, and his eyes grow wide, and he blushes and then stands up and walks with Julia onto the dance floor. "Okay pal," Robbie says into the microphone, "Have fun!" and the depressed kid who was used to never being chosen for anything ever enjoys a dance with the gorgeous Julia Sullivan who had chosen to dance with him.

The second illustration is from the recent 2018 NFL Draft. In the fifth round the Seattle Seahawks drafted Shaquem Griffin from the University of Central Florida. Griffin is an outstanding linebacker, and he only has one hand. When he was only four years old, he had a medical condition that required the amputation of his left hand. And yet, he has proven to be a great football player, as he demonstrated when UCF defeated Auburn in the 2018 Peach Bowl (sorry, Auburn fans).

And it gets better. Against incredibly high odds Griffin was not only chosen to play at football's highest level, he was chosen to play on the same NFL team—and there are thirty-two NFL teams—as his twin brother Shaquill. How cool is that? When I was doing my daily ESPN online devotions the other day, I ran across an article about this by Brady Henderson, who writes:

> The scenario—Shaquem not only overcoming the longest odds to reach the pros, but also rejoining his twin brother on the same team—is the stuff of Hollywood movie scripts, not NFL reality. "I had a feeling (it could happen)," Shaquem said, "but the chances were really low"… Shaquem said the first thing (his brother) asked him after he got the call from the Seahawks was, "So are you living with me or not?" "We may have to knock some walls down," Shaquill joked on the conference call, "but we'll figure it out."

Brady writes, "To be sure, the Seahawks wouldn't have drafted Griffin if they didn't believe he could help their team, but this almost-too-good-to-be-true story comes at a time when Seattle could really use one" (April 30, 2018).

Like the fans in Seattle, perhaps you too could use an "almost-too-good-to-be-true story" that defies all odds—and the gospel of God's unconditional love for you in Jesus Christ is exactly that.

The Apostle Paul personally experienced this as God chose him, a violent blasphemer and persecutor of Christians, to preach the gospel throughout the Roman world, and write thirteen of the twenty-seven books of the New Testament. The same is true for you, as Paul wrote to the Corinthians:

> God chose what is foolish in the world to shame the wise; God chose what is weak in the world to shame the strong; God chose what is low and despised in the world, things that are not, to reduce to nothing things that are, so that no one may boast in the presence of God (1 Corinthians 1:27-29).

More recently, God chose a Catholic priest who fell in love and got married (and was therefore no longer a Catholic priest), a lifelong alcoholic who later got divorced, whose life was riddled was bad choices and the consequences of those choices (perhaps like your life). He was the late Brennan Manning, whom God chose against all odds to be a phenomenal preacher and writer. Like Paul, Brennan Manning personally experienced the unconditional love of Jesus Christ who had chosen him. Listen to how he describes this love in his book *Lion and Lamb*:

> God loves you as you are and not as you should be! Do you believe this? That God loves you beyond worthiness and unworthiness, beyond fidelity and infidelity, that He loves you in the morning sun and the evening rain, that He loves you without caution, regret, boundary, limit, or breaking point? I am not asking: Do you believe in love? That is abstract ideology... What I am asking is: can you say with conviction what the apostle John writes in his first letter: "I have come to know and believe in the love God has for me"? (20).

Think about your own life for a moment. Perhaps you can relate to Dylan McWilliams, because against all odds in your life you have been metaphorically attacked by a shark *and* bitten by a bear *and* stung by a rattlesnake. Or, like the sad boy at the bar mitzvah, you are used to never being chosen for anything, ever, because as the mean girl told him, "I don't dance with losers." Or, like Shaquem Griffin, you have suffered a tremendous loss of some kind and have hoped to still be chosen to play at the next level. Or, like the Apostle Paul, you have been a blasphemer who has dismissed Christianity as folly. Or, like Brennan Manning, you have suffered from addiction and broken relationships.

The good news of the gospel is that Jesus' words to his disciples at the Last Supper are his words to you today, "You did not choose me, but I chose you." In spite of all the wrong choices you have made, and the consequences of those choices, your eternal destiny will not be shaped by any of that. Instead, your eternal destiny will be shaped by the unconditional love of Jesus Christ, who has chosen you, who loved you so much that he gave his life for you on the cross to atone completely for all your wrong choices, and to secure for you a destiny of eternal life.

Against all odds, Jesus has smiled at you and asked you to dance. Against all odds, Jesus has drafted you to play on his team, the church, a team that has all your brothers and sisters who like you, against all odds, have been chosen by him. Again, at the Last Supper Jesus assured his disciples, "No one has greater love than this, to lay down one's life for one's friends," and the very next day on the cross he did exactly that. This "almost-too-good-to-be-true" gospel is absolutely true.

And even now, against all odds, the Risen Jesus offers that same love to you.

Amen.

You Have Eternal Life

God gave us eternal life, and this life is in his Son. Whoever has the Son has life; whoever does not have the Son of God does not have life. I write these things to you who believe in the name of the Son of God, so that you may know that you have eternal life (1 John 5:11-13).

In the Name of the Father, Son, and Holy Spirit.

On this Mother's Day, I am preaching a sappy sermon about mothers, with no apologies. Being a mother is the hardest, most demanding job on the planet. There is no close second. After literally having their growing child living in their bodies twenty-four hours a day, one hundred sixty-eight hours a week, for eight or nine months, mothers give painful birth to their child, which never leaves their bodies the same. And then, of course, a mother's job is only just beginning.

Children require twenty-four-hour-a-day care. They never stop eating, never stop needing things (especially clothes), and never stop making messes, ever. That isn't enough, so add rides to school and the doctor and sports practice and the orthodontist, add PTA meetings and helping with homework and hugging them when a bully makes them cry, add birthday parties and holiday traditions and trying not to engage with the never-ending one-upping with other mothers, and add thousands of other demands. Regardless of whether or not a mother also has a job outside her home, regardless of how many children a mother has, children, like nature, abhor a vacuum. Any vacuum of time, money, or energy will be immediately filled by needy children. It is no wonder that I once heard a mother make the following request: "I'll have a café mocha vodka valium to go, please!"

My mom managed to rear me without ever being committed to an institution, which in and of itself is proof to me that not only was she a great mom but that there must be a God. One of my favorite memories of my mom happened on my sixteenth birthday. She let me skip school, which itself was a great present, and took me to the DMV so I could get my driver's license. Then she took me to lunch and gave me my birthday present, a dual cassette boom box with auto reverse and dubbing capabilities. For a sixteen-year-old in 1984, it could not get any better than that.

Sometimes fathers just don't cut it, and children want and need their mothers more. In his Netflix comedy special *Don't Never Give Up,* Kevin James tells a story about his youngest daughter:

> Our little new one, she's not a daddy's girl right now. I wish she was. The other day she was crying, standing in the hallway late at night. I told my wife, "Let me go deal with this. It'll give me a chance to bond with her." So I walked down the hallway and I'm like, "What's the matter, sweetheart, is everything all right?" And she goes, "I want my mommy. I don't want you. Go downstairs." The first thing she said threw me the most… "I want my mommy," like, "I don't even know who the (heck) you are." Then, in case I'm confused, she makes it very clear: "I don't want you. I don't even want you on the same floor as me. You need to be a floor below me."

I am a big fan of Amy Poehler, who spent eight years on *Saturday Night Live* and then seven seasons on the hit comedy *Parks and*

Recreation. In her 2014 book *Yes Please,* she includes the following "poem and story" she wrote as a child:

> Parents although sometimes mad they get, I would always bet, that they do it from love. If so happens they punish you, and you wish you could punish them too, they do it out of love. They may yell at you and make you mad, but when they yell it makes them sad (I think). That's why parents are the best. Mine are better than all the rest. The end (204).

Among the many things Amy Poehler writes that her mother taught are: "Always have a messy purse… Dye your hair constantly… [and] Love your kids and hope they do better than you did" (204-205). Amy Poehler idolizes her mother.

Mothers often have to navigate very challenging circumstances that kids do not understand. In his 2006 book *For One More Day,* Mitch Albom writes about a middle-aged man named Charles Benetto whose life has fallen apart and who longs to spend one more day with his mom who had died years before. In one of the several episodes entitled "Times My Mother Stood Up for Me," Albom writes:

> It is three years after my father's departure. In the middle of the night, I awaken… My mother is suddenly in my room, whispering loudly, "Charley! Where's your baseball bat?" "What?" I grunt, rising to my elbows… "A bat," my mother says. "Why do you want a bat?" "Shhh!" my sister says, "She heard something." "A robber's in the house?" "Shhh!" my sister says. My heart races. As kids, we have heard of cat burglars (although we think they steal cats)…
>
> "Charley? The bat?" I point to the closet. My chest is heaving. She finds my black Louisville Slugger, and my sister lets go of her hand and jumps into my bed… My mother eases out the door. "Stay here," she whispers. I want to tell her that her grip is wrong. But she's gone… I hear footsteps. I imagine a big, ruddy

beast of a man coming up the stairs for my sister and me. Then I hear something real, a smash… I want to run downstairs. I want to run back to bed. I hear something deeper—is it another voice? A man's voice? I swallow. Moments later, I hear a door close. Hard. Then I hear footsteps approaching.

My mother's voice precedes her. "It's all right, it's all right," she is saying, no longer whispering, and she moves quickly into the room and rubs my head as she passes me to get to my sister. She drops the bat and it clunks on the floor. My sister is crying. "It's all right. It was nothing," my mother says. I slump against the wall. My mother hugs my sister. She exhales longer than I have ever heard anyone exhale before. "Who was it?" I ask. "Nothing, nobody," she says. But I know she is lying. I know who it was (91-93).

When it comes to your mother, some of you may echo Amy Poehler, who considers her mom "better than all the rest." Some of you may not. Or like Charles Benetto, maybe your mom looked out for you and protected you in ways that you barely understood—others of you, not so much. Some of you may have a strained relationship with your mother—or no relationship at all. And of course it can go the other way too, right? Perhaps you are a mother who wishes you connected more with your children or got along easier with them, or is weary of their resentment. Or perhaps you never wanted children or never had children, or you had them and wondered if they came with a return policy.

In the gritty 2017 coming-of-age film *Lady Bird,* Saoirse Ronan plays Christine "Lady Bird" McPherson, a senior in high school, who lives in a working-class neighborhood in Sacramento, California. She is at a thrift store with her mom with whom she has a strained relationship. They are looking for a prom dress. She emerges from a fitting room wearing a frilly pink dress and looking very happy. "I love it," she says, looking at her mom for approval.

"Is it too pink?" her mom asks. Lady Bird silently goes back into the fitting room, obviously upset.

"What?" her mom says. "Why can't you say I look nice?" Lady Bird replies. "I thought you didn't even care what I think." "I still want you to think I look good." "I'm sorry," her mom retorts; "I was telling the truth. Do you want me to lie?" "No, I just, I just wish that you liked me." "Of course I love you." Lady Bird emerges again from the fitting room, and looks at her mom: "But do you *like* me?" Her mom hesitantly replies, "I want you to be the very best version of yourself you can be." Lady Bird simply asks, "What if this *is* the best version?"

The grace of God, the actual gospel of God's unconditional love for you has nothing, absolutely nothing to do with your being "the best version of yourself you can be." In today's passage from the First Letter of John, the evangelist, the only one of Jesus' disciples who stood at the cross as Jesus suffered and died, is very to-the-point about what the gospel is all about:

> God gave us eternal life, and this life is in his Son. Whoever has the Son has life; whoever does not have the Son of God does not have life. I write these things to you who believe in the name of the Son of God, so that you may know that you have eternal life (1 John 5:11-13).

Jesus did not come to help you improve yourself, which is good news, because for many people, the older they get, the more entrenched they become in behaviors that are the exact antithesis of self-improvement. Jesus came to give life, eternal life. Jesus did not come to condemn the world, but to save the world. And the greatest mother in the history of the world, Jesus' mother Mary, played a vital role in this.

When the angel Gabriel told the young, engaged Mary that she would give birth to the Son of God, Mary's response was one of gentle humility and surrender: "Here am I, the servant of the

Lord; let it be with me according to your word" (Luke 1:38). As she carried Jesus in her womb, Mary had to endure the insults and gossip for carrying a child who was not Joseph's. Mary gave birth to Jesus in a barn, and her job was only just beginning. Mary nursed him, and was there when he took his first steps, when he spoke his first words. Mary knew every line of his hands and feet. Mary adored her son. When the twelve-year old Jesus had wondered off unbeknownst to her, Mary sought him until she found him in the temple, where Jesus asked her, "Did you not know that I must be in my Father's house?" (Luke 2:49). Being the mother of the Son of God was the hardest job in the world.

Mary witnessed much of Jesus' earthly ministry, saw his miracles, heard his preaching. Mary was even there at Calvary, where she stood up for her beloved son, and watched him suffer, the hands and feet she used to clean and coddle now nailed to a cross. And as Jesus' final breath drew near, Mary listened to Jesus ask John to look out for her. And after Jesus' chest finally stopped heaving, Mary heard her son exhale longer than she had ever heard anyone exhale before. And later Mary saw her resurrected Son, too. Mary was there all the way through.

Back to the film *Lady Bird* for a moment… Near the end of the film, as Lady Bird is unpacking and settling into her college dorm in New York City, she pulls out of her suitcase a manila envelope that is full of wrinkled, half-started letters from her mom, each of which begins the same way: "I love you so much and I don't know how to tell you that. I can't communicate it to you in a way that…"

The next scene she is on the phone with her father, who had salvaged all of his wife's incomplete, wadded-up letters from the trash and put them in their daughter's suitcase. He says, "She was worried that there would be errors, or mistakes or something, that you'd judge her writing abilities." "I wouldn't do that," Lady Bird replies. "I thought you should have them," her dad says; "I want you to know how much she loves you, but also don't tell her I salvaged them, okay?" "Okay." In the final scene of the film, Lady Bird calls and leaves a message for her mom:

> Hi Mom and Dad, it's me, Christine. It's the name you gave me. It's a good one. Dad, this is more for Mom. Hey Mom? Did you feel emotional the first time that you drove in Sacramento? I did, and I wanted to tell you, but we weren't really talking when it happened. All those bends I've known my whole life, and stores, and the whole thing. But I wanted to tell you I love you. Thank you.

Lady Bird let her mom off the hook—and the good news of the gospel is that God has let you, and your mother, and all us, off the hook as well. On this Mother's Day, the greatest mother ever, Mother Mary, would want you to know how much God loves you. You see, God knows every bend of the road in your life. God knows the whole thing, and God loves you unconditionally. So today may the Holy Spirit reassure your heart that, as John wrote, "You have eternal life."

Amen.

Where Your Strength Ends, God's Grace Begins

The Spirit helps us in our weakness, for we do not know how to pray as we ought, but that very Spirit intercedes with sighs too deep for words. And God, who searches the heart, knows what is the mind of the Spirit, because the Spirit intercedes for the saints according to the will of God (Romans 8:26-27).

In the Name of the Father, Son, and Holy Spirit.

Every year on Pentecost Sunday we celebrate the outpouring of the Holy Spirit. At the Last Supper Jesus promised his disciples that after his departure he would send the Holy Spirit, the "Advocate," the "Spirit of truth":

> When the Advocate comes, whom I will send to you from the Father, the Spirit of truth who comes from the Father, he will testify on my behalf... When the Spirit of truth comes, he will guide you into all truth" (John 15:26; 16:13).

Several weeks later, in Jerusalem, Jesus kept his promise, as Luke wrote:

> When the day of Pentecost had come, the disciples were all together in one place. And suddenly from heaven there came a sound like the rush of a violent

> wind, and it filled the entire house where they were sitting. Divided tongues, as of fire, appeared among them, and a tongue rested on each of them. All of them were filled with the Holy Spirit (Acts 2:1-4).

The same Holy Spirit who filled the disciples can fill you anew today—as Jesus said, "If you then, who are evil, know how to give good gifts to your children, how much more will the heavenly Father give the Holy Spirit to those who ask him!" (Luke 11:13). Have you ever asked God to fill you with the Holy Spirit?

As Jesus said, the Holy Spirit indeed leads you into all truth, and reminds you of what you so often forget—that you are loved unconditionally by the Creator and Redeemer of the universe, that the presence of the Living God is with you all the time, no matter what. And today I am preaching on a specific way the Holy Spirit ministers the grace of God in your life—as Paul wrote in today's epistle passage: "the Spirit helps us in our weakness" (Romans 8:26). There are times when you are so weak, so utterly in need of God's help that you do not even know how to pray. And yet that is exactly where the Holy Spirit meets you. Where your strength ends, God's grace begins. Paul put it this way:

> The Spirit helps us in our weakness, for we do not know how to pray as we ought, but that very Spirit intercedes with sighs too deep for words. And God, who searches the heart, knows what is the mind of the Spirit, because the Spirit intercedes for the saints according to the will of God (Romans 8:26-27).

Sometimes being weak is not so bad, like when you fall in love. Along those lines here are some lyrics from the beautiful Belinda Carlisle, former lead singer of the classic 80s rock band the Go-Go's. When I was in college, the only guys I knew who did not have a crush on Belinda Carlisle were either in serious denial or were just plain lying. In 1988, she had a huge hit called "I Get Weak," about what happens when we fall in love:

> I get weak when I look at you
> Weak when we touch
> I can't speak when I look in your eyes
> I get weak when you're next to me
> Weak from this love
> I'm in deep when I look in your eyes
> I get weak
>
> (From her 1987 album *Heaven on Earth*)

Each of you has experienced that kind of weakness. It is amazing isn't it?

But outside of that kind of weakness we live in a world that does not value weakness at all, a world in which we either need to overcome our weaknesses or disguise them. In job interviews when you are almost invariably asked, "What are your strengths and weaknesses?" you are supposed to disguise your weaknesses as actual strengths: "One of my weaknesses is that I can be impatient with those who are not as passionate about their work as I am, but I just really like to get things done," or "One of my weaknesses is that I tend to be a perfectionist, but I just want to see things done right." Disguising your weaknesses may work in job interviews, but in real life, and in real relationships, it ultimately backfires.

There are times when, try as you might, you cannot disguise your weaknesses; they are there for all to see. That is when you need the Holy Spirit to help you in your weakness. The good news is where your strength ends, God's grace begins.

Many years ago when I was in the process toward ordination, I was being interviewed (or interrogated) by a diocesan standing committee who asked the following two-part question that I never saw coming: "What is one of the greatest failures in your life, and how did you experience God's grace in that?" There was no getting around that question, because in our failures we actually experience the grace of God—because the Spirit helps us in our weakness.

That was not only the most important question I was asked that day, but also the only question I remember being asked, perhaps because it was the only question that related to real life and real ministry. Why? Because the grace of God connects with your life as it actually is, not as it could be or should be. The grace of God is especially powerful in your failures and weaknesses.

In the mid-twentieth century an Episcopal priest named Sam Shoemaker was instrumental in the formation of Alcoholics Anonymous, which has helped millions of people with addiction recovery. And where do the Twelve Steps begin? By acknowledging weakness: Step One is "We admitted we were powerless over alcohol—that our lives had become unmanageable," and Step Two is "We came to believe that a Power greater than ourselves could restore us to sanity." In other words, the Holy Spirit helps us in our weakness.

This is utterly contrary to the self-assured individualism that is ingrained in our culture, but it is true, especially when your self-assured individualism falls short. "The Lord helps those who help themselves"—that is the Law. "The Lord helps those who cannot help themselves"—that is the Gospel. This is not only true for members of Alcoholics Anonymous; it is true for all of us.

Jesus did not come for the righteous but for sinners. Jesus did not come for the healthy but for the sick. Jesus did not come for the found but for the lost. Jesus did not come for the strong, but for the weak. In his account of the gospel, Matthew wrote that crowds followed Jesus, crowds of sick and lost and weak sinners, because the Holy Spirit had anointed Jesus to help them in their weakness, because they knew that as the Old Testament prophet Isaiah had foretold centuries earlier, Jesus would "not break a bruised reed or quench a smoldering wick" (Matthew 12:20). Think about your life for a moment. Where are you bruised? Where is the flame that once burned so bright but is now a "smoldering wick"? Where are you sick, or lost, or weak? Again, that is where the grace of God meets you.

The church is not a club of self-made overachievers. The church is a fellowship of failures. Speaking for myself, I have an impressive array of weaknesses, and a fine assortment of failures, some of which are there for all to see. But I have experienced, again and again in my own life, that where I am the weakest, where I am the most in need of the help of the Holy Spirit—which the older I get is increasingly the rule rather than the exception—that is where the grace of God so often connects with my life, because "the Spirit helps us in our weakness."

They rarely teach that at seminaries. Instead, seminaries often try to "form" skilled professionals for the institutional church who will be inspiring leaders *and* profound preachers *and* insightful scholars *and* wise administrators *and* caring pastors *and* stirring liturgists—on and on it goes. In his prescient 1979 book *The Wounded Healer,* the late Catholic scholar Henri Nouwen warned:

> Everywhere Christian leaders have become increasingly aware of the need for more specific training and formation. The need is realistic, and the desire for more professionalism in the ministry is understandable. But the danger is that instead of becoming free to let the spirit grow, the future ministers may entangle themselves in the complications of their own assumed competence and use their specialism as an excuse to avoid the much more difficult task of being compassionate (42).

Reliance on anything but the help of the Holy Spirit in our weakness will ultimately backfire—not just for ministers, but for all of us. The Old Testament prophet Zechariah was very to-the-point about this—"Not by might, nor by power, but by my spirit, says the Lord of hosts" (Zechariah 4:14). Or again, as Paul wrote, "the Spirit helps us in our weakness."

Paul wrote from personal experience. In his most vulnerable letter, his Second Letter to the Corinthians, Paul wrote about a "thorn in the flesh," something that was even too big for him to handle:

> Three times I appealed to the Lord about this, that it would leave me, but he said to me, "My grace is sufficient for you, for power is made perfect in weakness." So, I will boast all the more gladly in my weaknesses, so that the power of Christ may dwell in me…for whenever I am weak, then I am strong (2 Corinthians 12:8-10).

According to this passage the primary way the Holy Spirit helps us in our weakness is with the grace of God—the one-way, unearned, unconditional, all-encompassing love of God, a love that scripture assures us surpasses any breadth or length or height or depth we could imagine, a love that "surpasses knowledge" itself (Ephesians 3:18-19), a love that never ends (1Corinthians 13:8), a love that helps us when we cannot help ourselves.

And every week here at Christ Church, this grace of God by which the Holy Spirit "helps us in our weakness" is offered in the gospel of God's grace preached and the sacrament of God's grace administered. "For by grace you have been saved through faith," scripture assures us, "and this is not your own doing; it is the gift of God" (Ephesians 2:8). When we receive the sacrament of Holy Communion, we receive the grace of God, because as we read in *The Book of Common Prayer,* sacraments are "effectual signs of grace, and God's good will towards us, by the which he doth work invisibly in us, and doth not only quicken, but also strengthen and confirm our Faith in him" (872).

Jesus never avoided "the much more difficult task of being compassionate." Jesus was moved with compassion, moved from heaven to earth, moved from the manger to the cross. Jesus never disguised his human weakness. Jesus came in the human weakness of a newborn baby, and died on the cross, his human weakness there for all to see. But "God's weakness is stronger than human strength... God chose what is weak in the world to shame the strong" (1 Corinthians 1:25, 27).

Jesus "was crucified in weakness, but lives by the power of God" (2 Corinthians 13:4). It was the power of the Holy Spirit that raised Jesus from the dead. And at the end of your life, when your human weakness will be there for all to see, and you die, you too will be raised. Your earthly body will be "sown in weakness...raised in power" (1 Corinthians 15:43), the power of the Holy Spirit.

Where your strength ends, God's grace begins. That is the good news of the gospel on this Pentecost.

Today, may the same Holy Spirit who filled the disciples fill you anew, and help you in your weakness.

Amen.

The Lord of the Sabbath

One sabbath he was going through the cornfields; and as they made their way his disciples began to pluck heads of grain. The Pharisees said to him, "Look, why are they doing what is not lawful on the sabbath?" And he said to them, "Have you never read what David did when he and his companions were hungry and in need of food? He entered the house of God, when Abiathar was high priest, and ate the bread of the Presence, which it is not lawful for any but the priests to eat, and he gave some to his companions." Then he said to them, "The sabbath was made for humankind, and not humankind for the sabbath; so the Son of Man is lord even of the sabbath" (Mark 2:23-28).

In the Name of the Father, Son, and Holy Spirit.

A few years ago *The Economist* posted a fascinating article entitled, "In Search of Lost Time: Why Is Everyone So Busy?" The article begins:

> "Our grandchildren", reckoned John Maynard Keynes in 1930, would work around "three hours a day"—and probably only by choice…Whizzy cars and ever more time-saving tools and appliances guaranteed more speed and less drudgery in all parts of life. Social psychologists began to fret: whatever would people do with all their free time? (December 20, 2014).

Twenty years later in 1950, *The Associated Press* made this prediction: "Tell your children not to be surprised if the year 2000 finds a 35-hour or even a 20-hour work week fixed by law." So this morning, in 2018, let me ask you, "How's your 20-hour work week going?" Technological advances have also created lots of free time for you, right? Not so much… Back to *The Economist* article:

> Everybody everywhere seems to be busy. In the corporate world, a "perennial time-scarcity problem" afflicts executives all over the globe, and the matter has only grown more acute in recent years… These feelings are especially profound among working parents. As for all those time-saving gizmos, many people grumble that these bits of wizardry chew up far too much of their days, whether they are moldering in traffic, navigating robotic voice-messaging systems or scything away at e-mail—sometimes all at once (December 20, 2014).

Can you relate? In spite of all these predictions of fewer work hours and all the technological advances and time-saving gadgets, the reality is that we are still pressed for time. And even more significantly, we are overworking ourselves on a pathological level. Several years ago, in an article for *Forbes* magazine, writer Melanie Haiken asked: "Would you leave the office at a decent hour if you knew that long hours at your desk could, quite literally, be killing you?" She continued:

> Studies in Denmark and England followed completely different groups of workers—with the only common denominator being a high stress factor—and came up with similar results. In England, British civil servants who worked more than ten hours a day were found to be 60 percent more likely to develop heart disease or have a heart attack than people who clock just seven hours a day… Meanwhile, a team following nurses in Denmark discovered that those who rated themselves as feeling "too much" pressure at work

had a significantly higher risk of developing angina or myocardial infarction…leading the researchers to point out that stress appears to override everything else (August 23, 2011).

In other words, the combination of being overworked and overstressed is literally deadly. I have presided at many funerals for people who died much younger than they could have because of overwork and overstress. At the funeral receptions, amidst the ubiquitous deviled eggs and chocolate chip cookies and ham biscuits and fruit punch, I hear about what "hard workers" these people were. Being a hard worker is great, but in the hundreds of deathbed visits I have done over the years, not once has anyone ever told me they wished they had worked more. They have shared many regrets with me, particularly about broken relationships in their lives that they wish weren't broken, but never the regret of not working more.

And yet we pride ourselves on working ourselves to death. In the classic television show *The Office,* Rainn Wilson played the neurotic Dwight Schrute, who prided himself as being a hard worker—so much so that he made a self-promotional poster featuring his picture with his name as an acrostic: "D-Determined, W-Worker, I-Intense, G-Good Worker, H-Hard Worker, and T-Terrific." We all know people like Dwight Schrute, and sometimes we ourselves are just like him.

When I was in college, I heard a preacher once proclaim: "Pray as if everything depended on God and work as if everything depended on you." That sounded great to an idealistic and driven twenty-year-old, and for years, I did just that—prayed as if everything depended on God and worked as if everything depended on me (and yes, sometimes I still revert to this). But this is not only dangerous and oxymoronic, it is also unbiblical. Scripture tells us, "Unless the Lord builds the house, those who build it labor in vain… It is vain that you rise up early and go late to rest, eating the bread of anxious toil" (Psalm 127:1-2).

Along these lines, the scriptures appointed for today are full of good news for the overworked and overstressed, good news for those whose diet often includes "the bread of anxious toil," good news for those who never seem to have enough time.

In the Old Testament book of Deuteronomy, Moses, nearing his death, recapitulated to Israel the law of God, including the most overlooked of the Ten Commandments: "Observe the sabbath day and keep it holy, as the Lord your God commanded you. Six days you shall labor and do all your work. But the seventh day is a sabbath to the Lord your God; you shall not do any work." Why did God command this? Because God had already done this most important work for Israel: "Remember that you were a slave in the land of Egypt, and the Lord your God brought you out from there with a mighty hand and an outstretched arm; therefore the Lord your God commanded you to keep the sabbath day" (Deuteronomy 5:12-15). Notice that none of the Ten Commandments has anything to do with work, because most of us overwork ourselves, but the fourth commandment has to do with rest, because most of us do not rest enough.

In today's gospel lesson, Jesus takes this a step further, as Mark wrote:

> One sabbath he was going through the cornfields; and as they made their way his disciples began to pluck heads of grain. The Pharisees said to him, "Look, why are they doing what is not lawful on the sabbath?" And [Jesus] said to them, "Have you never read what David did when he and his companions were hungry and in need of food? He entered the house of God, when Abiathar was high priest, and ate the bread of the Presence, which it is not lawful for any but the priests to eat, and he gave some to his companions." Then he said to them, "The sabbath was made for humankind, and not humankind for the sabbath; so

the Son of Man is lord even of the sabbath" (Mark 2:23-28).

The incident Jesus refers to here is from an Old Testament passage in which David, who had earlier killed Goliath and delivered Israel from the Philistines, was fleeing for his life, because King Saul was out to kill him. David went to Ahimelech the priest and asked for bread, and Ahimelech responded, "I have no ordinary bread at hand, only holy bread" and yet "the priest gave him the holy bread; for there was no bread there except the bread of the Presence" (1 Samuel 21:1-6).

In the midst of being overstressed and overworked, in the midst of the time of his life literally running out, David went the house of God for bread, and was freely given "the bread of the Presence." And that is what Jesus, the Lord of the Sabbath, offers you every week at church in Holy Communion. "The sabbath was made for humankind," Jesus said, "and not humankind for the sabbath." Your relationship with God is not a homework assignment (you already have enough homework assignments), your relationship with God is a gift from the Lord of the Sabbath.

On December 8, 1980, John Lennon, who had received much bad press for his recent reclusive lifestyle, was shot and killed outside of his apartment building in Manhattan. A few months later, my favorite song from his final album, *Double Fantasy*, a song entitled "Watching the Wheels," was posthumously released:

> People say I'm crazy doing what I'm doing
> Well, they give me all kinds of warnings to save me
>   from ruin
> When I say that I'm okay, well, they look at me
>   kind of strange
> "Surely, you're not happy now, you no longer play
>   the game"
>
> People say I'm lazy, dreaming my life away
> Well, they give me all kinds of advice designed to

> enlighten me
> When I tell them that I'm doing fine watching
> shadows on the wall
> "Don't you miss the big time, boy. You're no longer
> on the ball"
>
> I'm just sitting here watching the wheels go round
> and round
> I really love to watch them roll
> No longer riding on the merry-go-round
> I just had to let it go

God's commandment, to remember the sabbath and rest, is an invitation to step off the merry-go-round one day a week, to be reminded that your relationship with God, like your life itself, is a gift, not a homework assignment. When you work yourself to death, you forget that, and you find yourself on a never-ending treadmill that goes faster and faster, defies your time-saving gadgets, and leaves you feeling more and more stressed and more and more behind. The sabbath is a reminder that God is the one who keeps the world turning, not you. It is a commandment that offers not only rest, but also a restored perspective.

Jesus, the Lord of the Sabbath, was born in Bethlehem, which in Hebrew means "House of Bread." After his miracle of the feeding of the five thousand, Jesus proclaimed, "I am the bread of life… I am the living bread that came down from heaven. Whoever eats of this bread will live forever; and the bread that I will give for the life of the world is my flesh" (John 6:35, 51).

And on Good Friday, Jesus, the Bread of Life and the Lord of the Sabbath, did just that when he gave his flesh for the life of the world on Calvary. In same way God had delivered Israel from centuries of slavery in Egypt, with "a mighty hand and an outstretched arm," Jesus delivered you from the slavery of sin and death with his mighty hands nailed to a cross and his outstretched arms reaching out to a world working itself to death. And after his body rested in the tomb on the sabbath, Jesus was raised on Easter Sunday, because the Lord of the Sabbath is also the Resurrection and the Life.

You see, the good news of the gospel is that the most important work in the world, the atoning work of your eternal salvation, has already been done by Jesus Christ, the Lord of the Sabbath. And to help you remember that in a tangible way, Jesus instituted the sacrament of Holy Communion at the Last Supper—"This is my body that is for you. Do this in remembrance of me… This cup is the new covenant in my blood. Do this, as often as you drink it, in remembrance of me" (1 Corinthians 11:24-25).

In other words, you remember the sabbath and keep it holy by remembering the Lord of the Sabbath and his completed saving work for you, by receiving anew the Bread of Life, "the bread of the Presence."

So even as you climb back onto the merry-go-round, even as you continue to pray as if everything depended on God but work as if everything depended on you, even as you continue to eat "the bread of anxious toil," remember that the most important work of your eternal salvation has already been done by Jesus Christ.

And Jesus Christ, the Lord of the Sabbath, even now, beckons you, "Come to me all you that are weary and carrying heavy burdens, and I will give you rest" (Matthew 11:28).

Amen.

The Tender Love of Your Heavenly Father

For the love of Christ urges us on, because we are convinced that one has died for all; therefore all have died. And he died for all, so that those who live might live no longer for themselves, but for him who died and was raised for them. From now on, therefore, we regard no one from a human point of view; even though we once knew Christ from a human point of view, we know him no longer that way. So if anyone is in Christ, there is a new creation: everything old has passed away; see everything has become new! (2 Corinthians 5:14-17).

In the Name of the Father, Son, and Holy Spirit.

On this Father's Day I am preaching on the tender love of your Heavenly Father.

Father's Day is a joy for those who are close to their father, for those whose father was there for them—and perhaps taught them how to bait a fishhook or set up a campsite or throw a football or play a D-chord on a guitar, for those whose father not only loves them but likes them, for those whose father believes in them.

Last week I visited the Rock and Roll Hall of Fame in Cleveland, Ohio. It was an epic day. Last year one of my favorite bands, Journey, was finally inducted, and at the induction ceremony keyboardist Jonathan Cain said this:

> I want to begin by thanking my father, Leonard, for believing in me, my mentor, my vision keeper, who prophesied success from the time I was eight years old…and later said to me, "Son, don't stop believin'" on a life-changing phone call as I struggled with my career back in the 70s. He's gone now. I miss you, Dad, and I love you.

The tender love of his father, and that life-changing phone call from his father inspired Jonathan Cain to write Journey's biggest hit, the legendary song, "Don't Stop Believin'," an anthem that has resonated with millions of people.

One of my favorite comediennes is the hilarious Amy Poehler, who used to star on the TV shows *Saturday Night Live* and later *Parks and Recreation*. In her 2014 book *Yes Please,* she reveals the positive impact her father, William, had on her life: "For my wedding, my father, his friends, and my uncles performed a surprise tap-dance number with top hats and canes. He is generous, nosy, and good at arm wrestling" (202). Then Amy Poehler recounts some things her dad taught her: "Girls can do anything boys can do. Street smarts are as important as book smarts. Your mother is smarter than me and I am fine with it. You don't want to be the creepy dad. It's okay to cry. It's okay to argue. [And finally] Tell everyone you meet what your daughter does until your daughter asks you to stop" (206).

Father's Day is great for the Jonathan Cain's and Amy Poehler's of the world, but not so fun for those whose relationship with their father is, or was, strained or nonexistent, for those whose father was not there for them, whose father neither likes them nor loves them. In January, while driving to Oxford, I took a detour through Columbus, Mississippi, and visited the childhood home of the great playwright Tennessee Williams. Upstairs there is an impressive display of photographs and memorabilia documenting his life and work. One quote under a childhood family photo was particularly poignant: "Tennessee would spend his entire life regretting the lack of his father's love." That is a loaded sentence. And sadly, Tennessee Williams was and is not alone.

Many years ago I presided at a wedding for a couple in their early thirties. The bride was an Ivy League educated surgeon, an accomplished overachiever—very soft spoken and kind. Her first marriage had ended in divorce because her husband was abusive, and she had later fallen in love with a fellow doctor. She was thrilled about getting remarried, thrilled about having a second chance. During the premarital counseling, she shared about her strained relationship with her father, and how his mere presence caused her to become flustered and insecure. Just prior to the wedding rehearsal I saw this firsthand. She was not herself at all.

Her father pulled me aside into the narthex and began ranting about his daughter and how angry he was about her divorce because no one in the history of their distinguished family had ever been divorced. He looked at me angrily: "You're a priest. Tell me what you would do about this!" I asked, "Do you really want to know?" He leaned in closer. "Yeah." "I would give your daughter a hug and tell her that you love her and that you wish her all the best." He shook his head at me: "I can't believe you condone this," and walked away. And indeed at the wedding rehearsal and wedding his brilliant daughter was not herself. Even the most accomplished are not immune to father issues.

And unfortunately it is common for those who have been wounded by their earthly father to view their Heaven Father through that same lens. But your Heavenly Father loves you more than you could imagine with an unconditional love, with no ulterior motives, no strings attached, no catch. Scripture assures us, "See what love the Father has given us, that we should be called children of God; and that is what we are… Beloved, we are God's children now" (1 John 3:1-2).

In today's passage from his most vulnerable letter, his Second Letter to the Corinthians, the Apostle Paul writes about this tender love of God:

> For the love of Christ urges us on, because we are convinced that one has died for all; therefore all have died. And he died for all, so that those who live might live no longer for themselves, but for him who died and was raised for them (2 Corinthians 5:14-15).

Then Paul takes it a step further:

> From now on, therefore, we regard no one from a human point of view; even though we once knew Christ from a human point of view, we know him no longer that way. So if anyone is in Christ, there is a new creation: everything old has passed away; see everything has become new! (2 Corinthians 5:16-17).

Do you believe that? Do you believe that out of his tender love your Heavenly Father sent his Son Jesus to die on the cross for you? Do you believe that your Heavenly Father does not regard you from a human point of view, but rather from a divine point of view of tender love, a divine point of view that sees you as a new creation, a divine point of view that makes everything new? Do you believe that?

That sounds too good to be true, but it is true, because it is the gospel. Every year on Palm Sunday we pray, "Almighty and everliving God, in your *tender love* for the human race you sent your Son our Savior Jesus Christ to take upon him our nature and to suffer death upon the cross" (*BCP* 219, italics added). On Good Friday, God was not concerned about the distinguished reputation of your family (or the lack thereof); God was concerned about you—and still is. The tender love of your Heavenly Father for you has never changed.

In his 1994 book *Abba's Child*, the late preacher and writer Brennan Manning recounted how receiving this tender love from our Heavenly Father changed the trajectory of his life. In January 1977 he went on a silent retreat and struggled, or as he put it, he was "scatterbrained, disoriented, rowing with one oar in the water." But something happened after a night of prayer, as he wrote: "At ten minutes after five the next morning I left the chapel with one phrase ringing in my head and pounding in my heart: *Live in the wisdom of accepted tenderness*" (64).

Let me repeat that: Live in the wisdom of accepted tenderness. He then defines the difference that accepting the tender love of your Heavenly Father can make in your life:

> The experience of a warm, caring, affective presence banishes our fears. The defense mechanisms of the imposter—sarcasm, name-dropping, self-righteousness, the need to impress others—fall away. We become more open, real, vulnerable, and affectionate. We grow tender (64).

In other words, accepting the tender love of your Heavenly Father will eventually bear the fruit of tenderness in your life. But even if you refuse the tender love of your Heavenly Father, his love for you still remains unchanged. In perhaps the most gospel-soaked of Jesus' parables, the Parable of the Prodigal Son, Jesus depicts this unchanging tender love of your Heavenly Father. The younger of a wealthy man's two sons demands his inheritance and squanders all of it, until he hits rock bottom. Jesus describes what happened next:

> So he set off and went to his father. But while he was still far off, his father saw him and was filled with compassion; he ran and put his arms around him and kissed him. Then the son said to him, "Father, I have sinned against heaven and before you; I am no longer worthy to be called your son." But the father said to his slaves, "Quickly, bring out a robe—the best one—and put it on him; put a ring on his finger and sandals on his feet. And get the fatted calf and kill it,

Grace to Help in Time of Need

and let us eat and celebrate; for this son of mine was dead and is alive again; he was lost and is found!" And they began to celebrate (Luke 15:20-24).

And let me let you in on a secret: the celebration continues even now.

One more illustration…Like millions of others I am big fan of *Star Wars*, which is replete with father issues, from Darth Vader revealing himself as Luke Skywalker's father in *The Empire Strikes Back* to Kylo Ren killing his father Han Solo in *The Force Awakens*. The author Ian Doescher has rewritten the *Star Wars* films in Shakespearean English. Each volume of his "William Shakespeare's Star Wars" series, like the bard's plays, is divided into five acts and employs iambic pentameter and other literary devices. In *The Force Doth Awaken,* listen to how Ian Doescher renders the heartbreaking scene of Kylo Ren, who has pledged himself to the Dark Side as his father, Han Solo, bids his lost son to come home:

> Han: Come, return unto thy home.
>   We miss thy gentle presence in our lives.
>   'Tis not too late—'tis never too late, my son.
>
> Kylo: I do confess that I am torn asunder.
>   From all this pain I fain would be set free.
>   I know what I must do, yet fear I've not
>   The strength to make it so. O wilt thou help?
>
> (Kylo Ren reaches to hand Han his lightsaber)
>
> Han: Of course, whate'er thou wishest, my sweet boy—
>   Thou bring'st and e'er did bring me such great joy.
>
> Kylo (aside): Beyond the chamber dies the light outside,
>   An 'twere the light within my very soul—
>   Thus in my core doth darkness reign at last.

> (Kylo Ren turns on his lightsaber and runs Han through)
>
> But listen to what Han says to his son who has just mortally wounded him:
>
> Han: My son, whose face is still so dear to me—
> O, how I see thy mother still in thee (142-143).

Han Solo's tender love for his son, Kylo Ren, literally cost him his life, and yet even as he died, his tender love for his son remained unchanged—"my son, whose face is still dear to me." That mirrors the tender love of your Heavenly Father for you. No matter what, your face is still dear to your Heavenly Father.

Regardless of your earthly father's human point of view toward you, or your human point of view toward your earthly father, scripture is clear that the divine point of view of your Heavenly Father toward you is one of tender love.

So on this Father's Day, "Don't stop believin'" because the gospel is all about second chances and coming home and celebrations and God making everything new.

Don't stop believin' because the gospel is all about the tender love of your Heavenly Father for you.

Amen.

The Sure Foundation of God's Lovingkindness

On that day, when evening had come, he said to his disciples, "Let us go across to the other side." And leaving the crowd behind, they took him with them in the boat, just as he was. Other boats were with him. A great windstorm arose, and the waves beat into the boat, so that the boat was already being swamped. But he was in the stern, asleep on the cushion; and they woke him up and said to him, "Teacher, do you not care that we are perishing?" He woke up and rebuked the wind, and said to the sea, "Peace! Be still!" Then the wind ceased, and there was a dead calm. He said to them, "Why are you afraid? Have you still no faith?" And they were filled with great awe and said to one another, "Who then is this, that even the wind and the sea obey him?" (Mark 4:35-41).

In the Name of the Father, Son, and Holy Spirit.

In the collect for today, we are reminded of the gracious sovereignty of God: "O Lord…you never fail to help and govern those whom you have set upon the sure foundation of your lovingkindness" (*BCP* 230). This is very good news, especially in the seasons of our life when the foundations are shaken, or worse—when as the psalmist asked, "When the foundations are being destroyed, what can the righteous do?" (Psalm 11:3, *BCP* 596).

In today's gospel passage Mark recounts an episode when the

disciples felt like their foundations were being destroyed:

> When evening had come, Jesus said to his disciples, "Let us go across to the other side." And leaving the crowd behind, they took him with them in the boat, just as he was. Other boats were with him. A great windstorm arose, and the waves beat into the boat, so that the boat was already being swamped. But he was in the stern, asleep on the cushion; and they woke him up and said to him, "Teacher, do you not care that we are perishing?" (Mark 4:35-38).

Can you relate? Have you ever found yourself metaphorically doing what you are sure God called you to do, only to feel like your foundations are being destroyed due to something beyond your control? After all, it was not the disciples' idea to get into the boat and cross the lake that night, it was Jesus' idea. Moreover, the disciples had no control over the weather (do you have control over the "weather" in your life?), and still they found themselves in the midst of a violent storm—again, as Mark writes, "A great windstorm arose, and the waves beat into the boat, so that the boat was already being swamped." And yet, Jesus was with them: "just as he was," asleep in the stern. The disciples thought, even though Jesus was with them, that he was apparently indifferent, that he just did not care, which is why they awoke him and asked, "Teacher, do you not care that we are perishing?"

In your life each one of you has found yourself in violent storms, violent storms which you did not see coming, over which you had no control, during which you may have known intellectually that Jesus was present but felt emotionally he was not, or that if he were, he was indifferent or did not care. In his 1976 hit "The Wreck of the Edmund Fitzgerald," about the tragic November 10, 1975 sinking of a freighter during a violent storm on Lake Superior, Canadian singer-songwriter Gordon Lightfoot asked this: "Does anyone know where the love of God goes when the waves turn the minutes to hours?" (from the album *Summertime Dream*).

These storms take various forms, from a major financial setback, to a sudden job loss, to a broken relationship or divorce, to an unexpected medical diagnosis, to the death of a loved one, a veritable buffet of storms. And during such storms it is tempting not only to think God is absent, but also in cynical moments, that life itself is simply a joke, as Herman Melville wrote in his masterpiece *Moby Dick:*

> There are certain queer times and occasions in this strange mixed affair we call life when a man takes this whole universe for a vast practical joke, though the wit thereof he but dimly discerns, and more than suspects that the joke is at nobody's expense but his own... That odd sort of wayward mood I am speaking of, comes over a man only in some time of extreme tribulation; it comes in the very midst of his earnestness, so that what just before might have seemed to him a thing most momentous, now seems but a part of the general joke (Bantam Classics edition 243-244).

Along these lines, in his prescient song "All Along the Watchtower," Bob Dylan wrote about a conversation between a thief and a joker:

> "There must be some kind of way out of here," said
>   the joker to the thief
> "There's too much confusion, I can't get no relief"

How does the thief respond?

> "No reason to get excited," the thief, he kindly
>   spoke
> "There are many here among us who feel that life is
>   but a joke
> But you and I, we've been through that, and this is
>   not our fate
> So let us not talk falsely now, for the hour is getting
>   late"

(From his 1967 album *John Wesley Harding*)

Bob Dylan is exactly right—even though the storms in your life may tempt you dismiss life as a joke, that is not your fate, and so you need to be reminded of the truth of the gospel, the truth of the sovereign grace of God in the midst of those storms in your life, for indeed "the hour is getting late."

Last spring, I visited the Museum of Modern Art in New York City. I knew I would be moved seeing Van Gogh's "The Starry Night" (1889) and Picasso's "The Blind Man's Meal" (1903)—both of which are remarkable paintings, but I was unexpectedly moved by Jackson Pollock's 1947 drip painting entitled "Full Fathom Five." From a distance it looks like a simple mixture of dripped black, white, and gray paint, very chaotic, but when you look at it closely you see not only many other colors, but also something I had never seen before in any other painting, an assortment of detritus including nails, cigarette butts, a key, buttons, coins, matches—all actual objects embedded in the painting—resembling the flotsam and jetsam in the wake of a storm.

In fact, the title of this painting, "Full Fathom Five," is from Shakespeare's play about a storm at sea, *The Tempest*, in which the sprite Ariel sings this to Ferdinand, about his father Alonso's apparent death in that storm at sea:

> Full fathom five thy father lies;
> Of his bones are coral made;
> Those are pearls that were his eyes:
> Nothing of him that doth fade,
> But doth suffer a sea-change
> Into something rich and strange
> Sea nymphs hourly ring his knell
>   (I, ii, 396-402).

At that point in the play Ferdinand is convinced that his father, with whom he was very close, had been lost at sea, that his foundations were being destroyed. But the play was not over yet.

And Mark's account of the storm at sea did not end with the disciples crying to Jesus, "Do you not care that we are perishing?" This episode did not end with Jesus staying asleep and all of them sinking and dying. And this is also true with the violent storms in your life. Here is how the episode actually ended:

> [Jesus] woke up and rebuked the wind, and said to the sea, "Peace! Be still!" Then the wind ceased, and there was a dead calm. He said to them, "Why are you afraid? Have you still no faith?" And they were filled with great awe and said to one another, "Who then is this, that even the wind and the sea obey him?" (Mark 4:39-41).

This episode did not end with the disciples dying at sea, but with Jesus saving them. And Jesus made sure they got where they needed to go—as scripture tells us that after that storm "they came to the other side of the sea" (Mark 5:1). Not only does the Lord care about the storms in your life, not only is the Lord with you in those storms, ultimately the Lord will rescue you and save you and ensure that you get to "the other side of the sea." You have been set on the sure foundation of God's lovingkindness. Centuries before Jesus, the psalmist described what the Lord did (and does) for those in the midst of a terrifying storm at sea:

> They mounted up to the heavens and fell back to the depths; their hearts melted because of their peril. They reeled and staggered like drunkards and were at their wits' end. Then they cried to the Lord in their trouble, and he delivered them from their distress. He stilled the storm to a whisper and quieted the waves of the sea. Then they were glad because of the calm, and he brought them to the harbor they were bound for (Psalm 107:26-30, *BCP* 748).

In other words, the gracious sovereignty of God has the last word, not the storm.

In his compelling 1997 book *The Perfect Storm,* Sebastian Junger recounts the horrific 1991 autumn storm at sea that occurred along the New England coast. Many were lost at sea in that storm, but not Karen Stimpson and Sue Bylander, who, although they lost their boat, were rescued by the Coast Guard. Listen to this:

> "When I got up into the helicopter I remember everyone looking in my and Sue's faces to make sure we were okay," says Stimson. "I remember the intensity, it really struck me... They'd take us by the shoulders and look us in the eyes and say, 'I'm so glad you're alive, we were with you last night, we prayed for you. We were worried about you'" (163).

Near the conclusion of his book, Junger makes this important observation:

> Anyone who has been through a severe storm at sea has, to one degree or another, almost died, and that fact will continue to alter them long after the winds have stopped blowing and the waves have died down...the effects of a storm go rippling outward through webs of people for years, even generations... nothing is ever again the same (219-220).

On Good Friday, Jesus underwent the most violent storm of all in his suffering and death on the cross—as wave after wave of pain and mockery swamped him, and these waves turned the minutes to hours. Jesus died, dismissed as the Joker between two thieves, with no way out of there. And in this storm, Jesus felt all alone as he cried, "My God, my God, why have you forsaken me?" And when the storm ended, Jesus' life ended, too, and the foundations of the world appeared to be utterly destroyed. And then Jesus' body was buried "full fathom five" in a tomb.

But on Easter morning Jesus experienced the sea-change of the resurrection, and his body was transformed "into something rich and strange," a risen and glorified Jesus whose body still bore the scars from his storm at sea on Good Friday.

Back to Shakespeare's *The Tempest* for a moment… Near the end of the play, it is revealed that Ferdinand's father Alonso was not dead after all. Prospero, the magician whose gracious sovereignty had been involved the entire play, summons everyone before him, freely bestows forgiveness and blessings on all, and then speaks these concluding words of the play:

> And my ending is despair
> Unless I be reliev'd by prayer
>   Which pierces so that it assaults
>   Mercy itself and frees all faults.
>   As you from crimes would pardon'd be
>   Let your indulgence set me free
> (Epilogue 15-20).

So when the foundations are being destroyed, what can the righteous do? Well, Jesus, the Righteous One, Mercy personified, died on the cross to save you. Jesus' indulgence has already set you free, already set you forever on the sure foundation of God's lovingkindness, and will set you safely on "the other side of the sea."

Amen.

Your Eternal Superlative

Blessed be the God and Father of our Lord Jesus Christ, who has blessed us in Christ with every spiritual blessing in the heavenly places, just as he chose us in Christ before the foundation of the world to be holy and blameless before him in love. He destined us for adoption as his children through Jesus Christ, according to the good pleasure of his will, to the praise of his glorious grace (Ephesians 1:3-6).

In the Name of the Father, Son, and Holy Spirit.

Today I am preaching on your eternal destiny.

As a kid perhaps you were asked this question, "What do you want to be when you grow up?" When I was really young, I wanted to be a fireman. I had a toy firetruck complete with a folding ladder, and I would pretend my action figures were trapped in a burning building (the living room couch), and I would pull up the toy firetruck, unfold the ladder and bring them all back to safety. A few years later, like most of my friends, I dreamed of being a professional football player on the Washington Redskins like one of my childhood heroes, the legendary Hall of Fame running back John Riggins.

High school yearbooks often include senior superlatives for both the present and the future—present superlatives like "Best

Looking" or "Best Sense of Humor" or "Most Athletic"—and future superlatives like "Most Likely to Succeed" or "Most Likely to Be a Millionaire" or "Most Likely to Travel the World." After many years of pastoral ministry, I think it would be fun to include more realistic superlatives like "Most Likely to Have a Midlife Crisis" or "Most Likely to Get a DUI" or "Most Likely to Marry a Gold Digger."

Some people know what their earthly destiny is, like Bono, the lead singer of U2. Last month, I visited the Rock and Roll Hall of Fame in Cleveland, Ohio, which includes a theater that plays concert footage. When I was there, they were playing footage of U2's 2009 hit "Magnificent," a worship song in which Bono sings:

> I was born to sing for you
> I didn't have a choice but to lift you up
> And sing whatever song you wanted me to…
> Only love, only love could leave such a mark
> Only love, only love can heal such a scar
>   (From their 2009 album *No Line on the Horizon*)

When you were young and people asked you what you wanted to be when you grew up, what did you say? When you were in high school, regardless of whether or not you were labeled with a senior superlative, how did you see your life unfolding? As you look at your life now, some of you may have reached where you thought your destiny would lead, while others of you may have had unexpected events that have left you wondering if you ever had any destiny at all.

While there are some people, like Bono, who know why they were born, many who have shared with me in pastoral counseling would identify with the sixteenth century French writer Jean de La Fontaine, who quipped, "One often meets their destiny on the road they took to avoid it." Or perhaps, when it comes to your earthly destiny, you can relate to what the rock band Talking Heads sang:

> You may find yourself living in a shotgun shack
> And you may find yourself in another part of the world
> And you may find yourself behind the wheel of a large automobile
> And you may find yourself in a beautiful house with a beautiful wife
> And you may ask yourself, "Well, how did I get here?"
> (From their song "Once in a Lifetime" on the 1980 album *Remain in Light*)

One of the recurring themes of the classic 1994 film *Forrest Gump* is the theme of destiny. Early in the film Forrest, as a young boy, asks his mom, "What's my destiny, Mama?" She replies, "You're gonna have to figure that one out for yourself." Later in the film, Lieutenant Dan, who thought he knew his destiny of dying in the glory of battle, instead finds himself having lost both his legs. Forrest, who was wounded while rescuing Lieutenant Dan, is with him in a VA hospital. In the middle of the night, Lieutenant Dan reaches up and pulls Forrest off his bed onto the hard hospital floor and begins ranting about his foiled destiny:

> Now you listen to me. We all have a destiny. Nothing just happens; it's all part of a plan. I should have died out there with my men! But now, I'm nothing but a cripple, a legless freak! Look at me! You cheated me. I had a destiny. I was supposed to die in the field with honor! That was my destiny! And you cheated me out of it! You understand what I'm saying, Gump? This wasn't supposed to happen. Not to me. I had a destiny.

Late in the film, Forrest says to his beloved Jenny, "Jenny, I don't know if Momma was right or if it's Lieutenant Dan. I don't know if we each have a destiny, or if we're all just floating around accidental-like on a breeze, but I think maybe it's both." Whether you relate to Bono or La Fontaine, or to the Talking Heads or

Lieutenant Dan, or maybe Forrest Gump, today's epistle lesson from Paul's Letter to the Ephesians contains very good news about your eternal destiny:

> Blessed be the God and Father of our Lord Jesus Christ, who has blessed us in Christ with every spiritual blessing in the heavenly places, just as he chose us in Christ before the foundation of the world to be holy and blameless before him in love. He destined us for adoption as his children through Jesus Christ, according to the good pleasure of his will, to the praise of his glorious grace (Ephesians 1:3-6).

This passage is a loaded with high-octane gospel. Regardless of the choices you have made, some of which may have permanently impacted your earthly destiny, your eternal destiny is based on the choice God made when he chose you "in Christ before the foundation of the world." God has destined you to be adopted as one of his children. Why? Because God wanted to do so—or again, as Paul wrote, because of "the good pleasure of his will, to the praise of his glorious grace."

Elsewhere Paul similarly wrote to the Thessalonians about their eternal destiny, "God has destined us not for wrath but for obtaining salvation through our Lord Jesus Christ, who died for us, so that whether we are awake or asleep we may live with him" (1 Thessalonians 5:9-10). God has chosen you and destined you to eternal life. At the Last Supper, Jesus could not have been clearer about this when he said to his disciples, "You did not choose me but I chose you. And I appointed you to go and bear fruit, fruit that will last" (John 15:16).

I have experienced this in my own life. After I realized being a professional football player was not in the cards, I unexpectedly felt called to the priesthood when I was in sixth grade. I actually wrote about it in a "What I Want to Be When I Grow Up" essay that year. My sixth-grade teacher, Mrs. Cole, my favorite teacher ever, scribbled a note to my parents on the top of that essay along the lines of "I encourage you to pay attention to this because in my many years of assigning this essay I have never had anyone write about wanting to be a priest."

I held on to that desire to be a priest until my senior year in high school when I got into serious trouble at the little private school I attended, and I was expelled. My senior year was a total nightmare, and my senior superlative was a unique one: "Most Expelled." I went away to college, still thinking about the priesthood, but feeling like I was damaged goods and therefore disqualified. I thought I had forever ruined what I had thought would be my earthly destiny.

But over the course of many years, God brought much healing in my life, and because God is a God of grace, because God is a God of second chances (and third chances, and fourth chances, and all the chances you will ever need), I was eventually ordained a priest after all. And along the way I learned that I was by no means the only person who had considered themselves damaged goods and therefore ruined their earthly destiny. There are actually a lot of people in that club; it's a very, very big club.

Yes, your choices impact your earthly destiny (you know that), but when it comes to your eternal destiny, God's choice overrides your choice. You did not choose God, but God chose you "in Christ before the foundation of the world," God chose you "according to the good pleasure of his will, to the praise of his glorious grace." Your eternal destiny is one of eternal life through the grace of God in Jesus Christ. In Article 17 of the Thirty-nine Articles, the sixteenth-century distillation of Anglican Church doctrine, we read this:

> Predestination to Life is the everlasting purpose of God, whereby [before the foundations of the world were laid] he hath constantly decreed by his counsel secret to us, to deliver from curse and damnation

those whom he hath chosen in Christ out of mankind, and to bring them by Christ to everlasting salvation (*BCP* 871).

This idea of predestination makes some people uncomfortable or even cynical—like it makes no difference what choices we make because we are all puppets on puppet strings controlled by some universal puppeteer. There is even a theological tenet, supralapsarianism, held by some that God intentionally creates some people in order to damn them eternally to God's glory. But this does not line up at all with the gospel set forth in today's epistle passage, upon which Article 17 is based. Anglican scholar John Rodgers observes:

> There is no teaching of predestination to hell in Article 17 or in Scripture. Hell is a destiny mankind has chosen for itself in the Fall… To teach that God created persons in order to condemn them, so as to have occasion to reveal his justice, is foreign to Scripture, dishonors God, and is a false doctrine. Predestination to life…is good news for sinners (*Essential Truths for Christianity* 337).

Jesus' earthly destiny was one no one would have expected for the Son of God, whom you would think would have been destined to grow up in unimaginable privilege and receive the best education in the world and be a mighty military leader who would lead a successful revolt to free Israel from their Roman oppressors and then have a successful political and philanthropic career.

But Jesus' earthly destiny did not include any of that. Jesus spent his time with sinners—damaged goods who thought their bad choices had ruined their destiny. About his earthly destiny, Jesus said, "The Son of Man came not to be served but to serve, and to give his life as a ransom for many" (Mark 10:45); "The Son of Man came to seek out and to save the lost" (Luke 19:10); "And I, when I am lifted up from the earth, will draw all people to myself" (John 12:32).

On Good Friday Jesus did not avoid the road to Calvary. Even as the world chose to crucify him, Jesus chose to forgive, "Father, forgive them, for they do not know what they are doing" (Luke 23:34). His disciples were heartbroken, "This wasn't supposed to happen." But it was supposed to happen. Jesus' earthly destiny was to die on the cross for you, not only to forgive you for all the wrong choices you have made, but to ensure your eternal destiny of eternal life and eternal love "according to the good pleasure of his will, to the praise of his glorious grace."

Regardless of how your earthly destiny goes, even if like Lieutenant Dan you have experienced things that were not "supposed to happen," even if your choices leave you as damaged goods, your eternal destiny has been secured by the One who chose you "before the foundation of the world." The scars of the Risen Jesus attest that "only love could leave such a mark…only love can heal such a scar."

In other words, God has given you your eternal superlative: "Most Loved."

Amen.

Jesus, Your Compassionate Shepherd

The apostles gathered around Jesus, and told him all that they had done and taught. He said to them, "Come away to a deserted place by yourselves and rest awhile." For many were coming and going, and they had no leisure even to eat. And they went away in a boat to a deserted place by themselves. Now many saw them going and recognized them, and they hurried there on foot from all the towns and arrived ahead of them. As he went ashore, he saw a great crowd; and he had compassion for them, because they were like sheep without a shepherd; and he began to teach them many things (Mark 6:30-34).

In the Name of the Father, Son, and Holy Spirit.

The collect for today is one of my favorites in the entire *Book of Common Prayer,* because it clearly identifies both the reality of our weakness and the even greater reality of God's compassion for us in the midst of our weakness. This collect beautifully describes God as "the fountain of all wisdom [who knows] our necessities before we ask and our ignorance in asking." In other words, we are so weak we do not even know how to pray. But God, the "fountain of all wisdom," already knows all that. And so, in this collect, we ask God: "Have compassion on our weakness, and mercifully give us those things which for our unworthiness we dare not, and for our blindness we cannot ask; through the worthiness of your Son Jesus Christ our Lord" (*BCP* 231).

Along these lines, I am preaching today on Jesus your Compassionate Shepherd.

In today's gospel passage, Mark writes about what happened with Jesus and his apostles during a particularly busy time:

> The apostles gathered around Jesus, and told him all that they had done and taught. He said to them, "Come away to a deserted place by yourselves and rest awhile." For many were coming and going, and they had no leisure even to eat (Mark 6:30-31).

Can you relate? Have you ever been so busy with so much "coming and going" around you that you could not even find time to eat? For some of you, this may be the rule rather than the exception. Some of us may occasionally even take pride in this: "I was so slammed today I didn't even have time to eat!" I know that you and I have never felt that pride—this is all theoretical, right? And yet Jesus' response to his overworked and out-of-breath and hungry disciples is a compassionate one: "Come away to a deserted place by yourselves and rest awhile." And as Mark continues, "They went away in the boat to a deserted place by themselves" (Mark 6:32). Introverts love this passage of scripture!

But then Mark continues, "Now many saw them going and recognized them, and they hurried there on foot from all the towns and arrived ahead of them. As he went ashore, he saw a great crowd" (Mark 6:33-34). In spite of Jesus' invitation to the apostles to come away to a deserted place and rest, the "coming and going" of many needy people awaited them. And yet, Jesus showed the crowd the same compassion he had shown the apostles, as Mark tells us, "He had compassion for them, because they were like sheep without a shepherd" (Mark 6:34).

For the sake of those who "were like sheep without a shepherd"

A Collection of Sermons

Jesus became a Compassionate Shepherd—and he still is.

In the psalm appointed for today, the classic Psalm 23, David writes of the Lord being his Compassionate Shepherd in a season that must have mirrored that of the weary and hungry apostles: "The Lord is my shepherd; I shall not be in want. He makes me lie down in green pastures and leads me beside still waters. He revives my soul" (*BCP* 612). Perhaps you need the Lord to revive your soul today.

And it is the same with you. When you are tired and stressed and so busy you cannot even find time to eat, when the pressures and the expectations and the needs with which you are inundated pull you in a hundred different directions, when you are not even sure how to pray, when you are faced with the reality that your strength is not enough, not even remotely enough, rather that you are in fact beset with weakness—you do not need a motivational speaker. You need a Compassionate Shepherd, and Jesus Christ is exactly that.

Nearly fifty years ago, there was a little music festival called Woodstock, which attracted over 400,000 weak sheep without a shepherd. One of the acts was a new group from Canada understatedly called The Band, who sang about compassion:

> I pulled into Nazareth, was feeling about half past dead
> I just need some place where I can lean my head
> Hey mister, can you tell me where a man might find a bed?
> He just grinned and shook my hand
> "No" was all he said
> Take a load off, Fanny, take a load for free
> Take a load off, Fanny, and you put the load right on me
> (From their 1968 album *Music from Big Pink*)

This song, "The Weight," is considered one of the most influential rock songs ever, and was written by guitarist Robbie Robertson who recounted in his 2016 autobiography *Testimony*:

> As a songwriter, "The Weight" was something I had been working up to for years. I just heard what I was looking for. The images, the stories I had been putting away in my imagination's attic, had been brought out into the light (301).

Several years ago, I was on a road trip and this song came on the CD player in my truck and I just kept playing it over and over, and I could feel the Holy Spirit giving relief to my tired spirit. If you want to bask in gospel goodness, I encourage you to watch The Band's performance of this song with The Staples Singers in Martin Scorsese's iconic 1978 concert film *The Last Waltz*. "The Weight" is a song that will always resonate, because it a song about compassion for the weak.

We all need compassion sometimes—actually, more than sometimes. One of my favorite memories of my father took place when I was sixteen. It was the summer of 1985, my first summer with a driver's license, and therefore, by definition, an epic summer. I had finished my first day at a summer job at a lawncare company, having worked extra hard, trying to make a good first impression. After spending the day mowing apartment complexes and riding in the bed of a pickup truck in the heat, I was filthy and bone-tired. On the way home, in my old Chevy, complete with a high-tech AM-only radio and manual air conditioning (you rolled down the windows), I ran out of gas. I could not believe it. This was in the stone ages before cell phones, and so I hiked to a gas station and put my last quarter in the pay phone (remember pay phones?) and called home.

When my father arrived, I expected a lecture about not noticing the gas gauge or the need to pay better attention and be more responsible. Instead, I received compassion. He just grinned at me:

"You look like you've had a long day." He filled his plastic red gas can, drove me to my old Chevy, emptied the gas can into it, led me back to the gas station and filled up my gas tank. Moreover, that gas station was a 7-Eleven, and so to top it off, he bought me a Slurpee and, grinning again, said, "See you at home." When I was out of gas in more ways than one, my father gave me compassion. I never forgot that.

In what I consider one of the most profound and accessible theological books of the late-twentieth century, *The Ragamuffin Gospel* (1990), the late Brennan Manning describes how the compassion of God, the grace of God, is often incongruent with what we actually experience in the American church. He wrote:

> Put bluntly, the American church today accepts grace in theory but denies it in practice. We say we believe that the fundamental structure of reality is grace, not works—but our lives refute our faith… Too many Christians are living in the house of fear and not in the house of love. Our culture has made the word *grace* impossible to understand. We resonate with slogans such as: "There's no free lunch." "You get what you deserve."

Manning continues:

> As I listen to sermons with their pointed emphasis on personal effort—no pain, no gain—I get the impression that a do-it-yourself spirituality is the American fashion. Though the Scriptures insist on God's initiative in the work of salvation—that by grace we are saved, that the Tremendous Lover has taken to the chase—our spirituality often starts with self, not God (16-17).

The truth is, do-it-yourself spirituality falls short. The truth is, we all run out of gas sometimes and need compassion on our weakness. And that is when the truth of the gospel shows us that Jesus, our Compassionate Shepherd, does exactly that.

Jesus was and is not only moved with compassion for the crowd of needy people in today's gospel reading; Jesus was and is moved with compassion for you. Jesus, "the fountain of all wisdom," indeed knows your necessities before you ask and your ignorance in asking. Jesus has compassion on your weakness.

In the Parable of the Prodigal Son, Jesus paints a vivid picture of what your Compassionate Shepherd is really like. You probably remember the story. A wealthy man has two sons, the dutiful firstborn and the entitled younger son. The entitled younger son demands his part of the inheritance and his father gives it to him, all of it. The younger son travels far away and squanders everything his father had given him, all of it, "in dissolute living." He ends up sick, filthy, broke, and feeding pigs—not exactly congruent with being from a family of privilege.

Jesus tells us that the younger son hit rock bottom—aka, ran out of gas in more ways than one—and only then decided to come home. Moreover, he had prepared a speech for his father: "Father, I have sinned against heaven and before you; I am no more worthy to be called your son." But Jesus tells us what unexpectedly happened when the prodigal son neared home: "While he was still far off, his father saw him and was filled with compassion; he ran and put his arms around him and kissed him."

The son gave his speech: "Father, I have sinned against heaven and before you; I am no longer worthy to be called your son." He may have expected a lecture about how he had disgraced his family, or about how he needed to be more like his dutiful older brother. But instead, his father started giving orders to throw a party to welcome his prodigal son home—a party to end all parties. Not only that, his father gave his son a robe that was typically given to the guest of honor, a ring that signified his restored place in the family, and sandals for his filthy blistered feet, because he was not a servant, but his beloved son. The prodigal son had not returned to a house of fear; he had returned to a house of love (Luke 15:11-24).

Recently discovered Greek texts of the New Testament add that even The Band showed up to the party and everyone joined in the chorus: "Take a load off, Fanny, take a load for free. Take a load off, Fanny, and put the load right on me." And yes, there were Slurpees aplenty, for everyone.

The gospel is good news for the weak, good news for those who have run out of gas and down to their last quarter, good news for those who have "pulled into Nazareth, feeling about half past dead." Jesus of Nazareth, your Compassionate Shepherd, was moved with compassion so much that on Good Friday, as he took the weight of the cross upon his shoulders, he took the weight of the sin of the world upon himself—including your sin, all of it.

And even now Jesus, your Compassionate Shepherd, mercifully gives you those things which for your unworthiness you dare not and for your blindness cannot ask—including compassion on your weakness. Even now, Jesus, your Compassionate Shepherd, beckons you, "Take a load off…and you put the load right on me."

Amen.

Psalms and Hymns and Spiritual Songs

Do not get drunk with wine, for that is debauchery; but be filled with the Spirit, as you sing psalms and hymns and spiritual songs among yourselves, singing and making melody to the Lord in your hearts" (Ephesians 5:18-19).

In the Name of the Father, Son, and Holy Spirit.

When it comes to Christians and drinking alcohol, there are lots of conceptions and misconceptions. When a priest, a minister, and a rabbi walk into a bar, the bartender usually asks, "What is this, some kind of joke?" As you know, the main difference between Presbyterians and Baptists is that, when Presbyterians see one another at the liquor store, they actually speak to each other—whereas Baptists will avoid each another or simply go to the drive-through. When it comes to Episcopalians and alcohol, there is some truth to the saying, "Where you find four Episcopalians, you will find a fifth"—the origin of the term "Whiskeypalians."

In today's passage, from his Letter to the Ephesians, the Apostle Paul wrote: "Do not get drunk with wine, for that is debauchery; but be filled with the Spirit, as you sing psalms and hymns and spiritual songs among yourselves, singing and making melody to the Lord in your hearts" (Ephesians 5:18-19). When it comes to "singing and making melody to the Lord in your hearts," I think of the legendary Queen of Soul, who died last week, Aretha Franklin.

Aretha Franklin was born in a small house in Memphis, Tennessee, in 1942. Right before her tenth birthday, her mother died of a heart attack. Nevertheless, she taught herself to play piano by ear, began singing in front of her church at age nine, and at age sixteen joined gospel singers who travelled with Martin Luther King, Jr. Ten years later at his funeral, with his widow Coretta Scott and their four young children in the front row, Aretha Franklin sang the gospel classic, "Precious Lord":

> Precious Lord, take my hand
> Lead me on, let me stand
> I'm tired, I'm weak, I'm alone
> Through the storm, through the night
> Lead me on to the light
> Take my hand, precious Lord
> Lead me home

In addition to being a phenomenal gospel singer, she had a stellar secular music career that spanned five decades. She sold over 75 million records, won 20 Grammys, was the first woman inducted into the Rock and Roll Hall of Fame in 1987, and ranked by *Rolling Stone* magazine as the number one singer of all time. In addition to "Respect" and "Chain of Fools," one of her biggest hits of the late 60s was a song written by Carole King, "(You Make Me Feel) Like a Natural Woman." In fact, at the 2015 Kennedy Center Honors, Aretha Franklin surprised Carole King when she walked onstage and sang this song, reducing many to tears and receiving a standing ovation before she even finished singing.

When you learn some of Aretha Franklin's backstory, that in addition to her mother dying before Aretha's tenth birthday, that she was frequently taken advantage of as a teenager, that she had her first child just after turning fourteen, that she dropped out of high school her sophomore year and had her second child at age sixteen, that she was physically abused by her first husband—when you learn all that, you understand why Aretha Franklin brought such soul to these classic lyrics:

> Looking out on the morning rain
> I used to feel so uninspired
> And when I knew I had to face another day
> Lord, it made me feel so tired
> Before the day I met you, life was so unkind
> But you're the key to my peace of mind…
> When my soul was in the lost and found
> You came along to claim it…
> You make me feel like a natural woman

"When my soul was in the lost and found, you came along to claim it"—that is the gospel. That is exactly what Aretha Franklin experienced in her life, and that is what Jesus Christ, our Precious Lord, does for all souls in the lost and found, including yours. Throughout his earthly ministry Jesus ministered grace to souls in the lost and found. To lepers who were not allowed to touch or be touched by anyone—imagine that, no hugs, no kisses, no embraces, no high-fives, no human touches of any kind, ever—Jesus gave grace as he touched and healed them. To the blind man sitting by the side of the road Jesus gave sight. To the widow whose only son had just died, Jesus gave her resurrected and healed son back.

To his followers who were hungry in the wilderness he multiplied a little bread and fish so that everyone could eat as much as they wanted. To the woman caught in adultery and embarrassingly dragged before him in the temple, Jesus said, "Neither do I condemn you; go and sin no more." Even to the Roman soldiers who nailed him to the cross, Jesus gave grace, "Father, forgive them, they do not know what they are doing"—a prayer for forgiveness for all souls in the lost and found.

For Mary Magdalene, a woman who like the young Aretha Franklin was used to being mistreated and objectified by men, Jesus cast out her demons, gave her a brand-new start, and chose her as the first woman to see him after his resurrection. The risen Jesus gave grace to doubting Thomas, showing him his scars as evidence of his love—and the risen Jesus grace to Peter, who was still wallowing in guilt for denying Jesus three times, fully restoring his position as the chief apostle.

As a new football season has just gotten underway, I have been reading a biography on legendary NFL Hall of Fame quarterback Joe Montana, whose nickname was "Joe Cool" because of his calm demeanor under pressure. Joe was also respected by his teammates because, although highly competitive, he gave them grace. This went all the way back to high school when in the fall of 1972 he was quarterbacking his Ringgold High School team in what would later be renamed Joe Montana Stadium, and he gave grace to a teammate, as Keith Dunnavant writes:

> Following a Ringgold touchdown, fullback Craig Garry trotted onto the field to relay the two-point conversion play from the head coach. In the excitement, Garry forgot the play. "I just went blank," Garry recalled. Many quarterbacks faced with such a situation would have called a time-out and jogged to the sideline. Not Joe Cool. "Joe didn't miss a beat," Garry said, "He just calmly called a play—a 36 slant pass—to me, threw it perfectly, I caught it, and we had our two points" (*Montana* 25-26).

Joe Montana did not yell at his teammate, or throw him under the bus with his coach; instead, he gave his teammate the opportunity to make the crucial play, instead he gave Garry grace. Incidentally, at Notre Dame Joe Montana also gave grace to the famous Daniel "Rudy" Ruettiger, whose story inspired the hit 1993 film *Rudy*: "'Montana was one of the ones who always showed me respect... encouraged me... He understood what it meant to struggle'" (*Montana* 42).

And there have been many occasions in my life when, just like fullback Craig Garry, my mind, too, has gone blank, and I metaphorically have forgotten the play call, but many times there have been Joe Montanas in my life who gave me grace. I'll give you one example. Several years ago when I had only been here a couple of months, it was my turn to lead the 7:00AM Thursday morning Eucharist, and I forgot to set my alarm. I awoke at 6:54, scheduled to lead the service in six minutes. I threw on my clericals, sprinted across the church property with my disheveled hair, spewing words that were not exactly "psalms and hymns and spiritual songs." But as I arrived at the sanctuary, late, the doors were already unlocked, the candles already lit, everything all set to go, courtesy of Father Peter Ingeman who did not miss a beat, who did not throw me, the new rector, under the bus for being late, but instead threw me a perfect pass, and gave me grace.

The truth is every single one of us finds ourselves in the lost and found, in need of someone to come along and claim us. And that is what Jesus Christ does. Jesus himself said, "[I] came to seek out and to save the lost" (Luke 19:10). Moreover, in seeking you out and saving you when you are lost, Jesus also claims you, Jesus also calls you by name: "Do not fear, for I have redeemed you; I have called you by name, you are mine" (Isaiah 43:1). The same Holy Spirit who gives you "psalms and hymns and spiritual songs" to sing to the Lord is the One who bears witness in your heart that you are one of God's children, that you have been not only found, but also claimed by God as one of his own (Romans 8:14-16).

And at the end of your life, you will be eternally claimed by the One who gave his life on the cross for you on Good Friday and was raised from the dead on Easter Sunday—and the same risen Jesus who gave grace to Thomas and Peter will give grace to you, and call you home.

This literally happened with one of our own, Tal Barnidge, who died last week. In talking with his widow, Norma, this past week she shared how several times during his final days at hospice he asked her to please bring him some clothes. "Why?" she would ask. "Because I'm going home," he would reply—and the last time he told her that, he raised his arms and eyes upwards and smiled, "Because I'm going home." And that is what happened last Sunday, when Jesus came to the lost and found to claim Tal Barnidge and take him home, where he has joined the heavenly chorus in singing "psalms and hymns and spiritual songs" to our Precious Lord.

And lest you think this is all make-believe or a myth, I tell you that I have heard many similar stories throughout many years of ministry. The gospel is not make-believe or a myth. The gospel is the very true good news of the very true grace of God in Jesus Christ, who comes to all of us in the lost and found, to claim us, each and every one.

Jesus knows your backstory, Jesus understands what it means to struggle, and Jesus claims you as his own.

Back to Aretha Franklin for a moment, and then I'll close… In January 1972, at New Temple Missionary Baptist Church in Los Angeles, she recorded the live gospel album *Amazing Grace*, which is the bestselling live gospel album of all time. The title track is a nearly eleven-minute-long version of "Amazing Grace," the classic hymn all about how Jesus Christ comes to those whose souls are in the lost and found to claim them, all about how through God's grace "I once was lost but now am found." Aretha's live version of "Amazing Grace" on this album will give you Holy Spirit goose bumps, trust me. Interestingly, she ends her version of the hymn with the penultimate verse. Instead of ending it with the "When we've been there many years, bright shining as the sun…" verse, she ends it, "Through many dangers, toils, and snares, I have already come; 'tis grace that brought me safe thus far, and grace will lead me home."

And that is the gospel. Grace will lead you home.

You have been and will be claimed at the lost and found by Jesus Christ, your Precious Lord who has already done that for Tal Barnidge, who has already done that for the Queen of Soul—and who one day will do that for you.

And you, too, will join the ever-growing heavenly chorus singing "psalms and hymns and spiritual songs" to the eternal glory of your Precious Lord.

Amen.

Good News for the Brokenhearted

The Lord is near to the brokenhearted and will save those whose spirits are crushed. Many are the troubles of the righteous, but the Lord will deliver him out of them all. He will keep safe all his bones; not one of them shall be broken (Psalm 34:18-20, BCP 629).

In the Name of the Father, Son, and Holy Spirit.

Today I am beginning by juxtaposing two hit songs about something that all of us experience in our lives at some point: a broken heart.

The first is a moving 1966 Motown hit by Jimmy Ruffin in which he asks a very important question: "What Becomes of the Broken Hearted?"

> As I walk this land of broken dreams
> I have visions of many things
> But happiness is just an illusion
> Filled with sadness and confusion
> What becomes of the broken hearted
> Who had love that's now departed?
> The roots of love grow all around
> But for me they come a-tumbling down
> Every day heartaches grow a little stronger
> I can't stand this pain much longer

> I walk in shadows searching for light
> Cold and alone, no comfort in sight
> Hoping and praying for someone to care
> Always moving and going nowhere
> What becomes of the broken hearted
> Who had love that's now departed?

The second song is a gem called "Only Love Can Break Your Heart" by classic rock icon Neil Young from his 1970 album *After the Gold Rush* in which he sings:

> When you were young and on your own
> How did it fell to be alone?
> I was always thinking of games that I was playing
> Trying to make the best of my time
> But only love can break your heart
> Try to be sure right from the start
> Yes, only love can break your heart
> What if your world should fall apart?

How old were you the first time you experienced a broken heart? I was blessed, or lucky, because I did not experience my first broken heart until I was seventeen. Many people have their heart broken at a much younger age. It was the spring of 1986 during my junior year of high school and I had been going out with a beautiful classmate for a really long time by high school standards: two whole months. I was crazy about her. All the clichés about being so in love that you can hardly sleep or eat, that you can't stop thinking about or daydreaming about that person, that you count down the hours until you will see their smile and hear their voice again, that you spend so much time on the phone that your ear literally hurts, so in love that their kiss melts you—all of these things had happened to me.

But on a Wednesday afternoon that May a friend of hers handed me a note during last period, my first "Dear John letter" that let me know our going out together was over. I was devastated, and remember the combination of hurt and anger I felt as I lay on my bed into the night, staring at the ceiling, wondering what I had done wrong.

And what Jimmy Ruffin and Neil Young sang about were not just topics in a song, they were realities in my life as I found myself wondering "what becomes of the brokenhearted," as I learned the hard way that indeed "only love can break your heart." And I wish I could say that was the only time my heart has ever been broken, but that is not the case—and I also wish I could say I have never broken anyone else's heart, but that is not the case either.

And our hearts can be broken not just by the end of a romantic relationship but by being betrayed by a family member or a friend. Perhaps the most famous scene in the classic 1974 film *The Godfather Part Two*, the first movie sequel ever to win the Oscar for Best Picture, was when Michael Corleone, played by Al Pacino, confronts his brother Fredo during a New Year's Eve party in Cuba. The clock has just struck midnight and the New Year has just begun. Confetti and streamers are flying and the drinks are flowing and people are cheering and hugging and kissing.

Michael walks up to Fredo in the middle of all this. For years Fredo, as the older of the two brothers, had resented Michael and had felt passed over regarding "the family business." And so Fredo had betrayed Michael who was almost killed as a result, and Michael had figured it out. While hugging Fredo, Michael speaks into his ear, "There's a plane waiting for us to take us to Miami in an hour. Don't make a big thing about it." Then he takes his brother's head in his hands and kisses him on the mouth and looks into his eyes and says, "I know it was you, Fredo. You broke my heart. You broke my heart." Fredo is stunned and stumbles away in fear while Michael stares him down.

Later in the film Michael, albeit in a soft-spoken way, lowers the boom:

> Fredo, you're nothing to me now. You're not a brother, you're not a friend. I don't want to know you or

what you do. I don't want to see you at the hotels. I don't want you near my house. When you see our mother, I want to know a day in advance, so I won't be there—you understand?

Then Michael walks away. Near the end of the film, after their mother has passed away, Michael takes his revenge and orders Fredo to be killed. You might say the Corleone family was slightly dysfunctional. While this is an extreme example from Hollywood, in many years of pastoral ministry I have seen betrayals in families that have resulted in broken hearts, bad blood, and even revenge being taken posthumously by leaving family members out of a will. There is a reason *The Godfather* films have resonated with people for over four decades.

Some of the greatest poets have also resonated because they too have experienced a broken heart. As he suffered from tuberculosis, John Keats, the great English Romantic poet, wrote in a letter to a friend, "I have coals of fire in my breast. It surprises me that the human heart is capable of containing and bearing so much misery. Was I born for this end?" (*Everyman's Library Pocket Poets: Keats* 257-248). He died on February 23, 1821. He was only twenty-five years old.

Think about your own life for a moment. When was the first time your heart was broken? Or the most recent time your heart was broken? Was it due to the breakup of a romantic relationship, or a divorce—your own or your parents' or your children's? Or was it due to a betrayal from a member of your family or a business partner? Some of you may have a broken heart right now.

So "what becomes of the broken hearted?" What do you do when you learn that "only love can break your heart"?

While the bad news is that you have already or will have your heart broken, today's psalm contains good news for the brokenhearted. Listen to this:

> The Lord is near to the brokenhearted and will save those whose spirits are crushed. Many are the troubles of the righteous, but the Lord will deliver him out of them all. He will keep safe all his bones; not one of them shall be broken (Psalm 34:18-20, *BCP* 629).

"The Lord is near to the brokenhearted and will save those whose spirits are crushed." Although when brokenhearted we may feel the most alone, we are not alone at all—the Lord is near. Throughout his earthly ministry Jesus drew near to the brokenhearted—bereaved widows, lepers, sinners, tax collectors, adulterers, prostitutes, mothers and fathers whose children were dying or dead, the deaf and the blind, the lost and the hungry, the rejected and the outcast—Jesus continually drew near to the brokenhearted and ministered grace and mercy and compassion and love and in doing so, saved "those whose spirits (were) crushed."

And at the Last Supper Jesus, whose heart was beginning to break, nevertheless had good news for the brokenhearted, as he assured his disciples, "Do not let your heart be troubled. Believe in God, believe also in me…do not let your hearts be troubled and do not let them be afraid" (John 14:1 and 27).

And you remember what happened later that night, as Jesus finished praying in the Garden of Gethsemane he was approached by a mob and betrayed by Judas, complete with a kiss. And Jesus' heart continued to break. And as he was falsely accused and beaten and mocked and forced to carry the instrument of his own death to the top of Calvary, Jesus' heart continued to break.

Unlike Michael Corleone, Jesus did not write off Judas or any of us, who have all betrayed the Lord in one way or another. Instead, Jesus died for us.

And as he suffered on the cross Jesus' spirit was crushed and he felt alone—"My God, my God, why have you forsaken me?" Moreover, he experienced what had been prophesied by the psalmist many centuries earlier: "Reproach has broken my heart, and it cannot be healed; I looked for sympathy, but there was none, for comforters, but I could find no one…when I was thirsty, they gave me vinegar to drink" (Psalm 69:22-23).

And as his heart continued to break Jesus in fact said, "I am thirsty," and was indeed given vinegar to drink (John 19:28-29).

And then Jesus' heart finally broke, and he died for all the broken hearted.

And not only were God the Father and God the Holy Spirit near Jesus the Righteous Son as his heart broke on Good Friday, Jesus was raised from the dead on Easter Sunday just as we also read in today's psalm, "Many are the troubles of the righteous, but the Lord will deliver him out of them all."

And after Jesus' death on the cross John records that when the soldiers came to break Jesus' legs to expedite his death and saw that he had already died, that "Instead, one of the soldiers pierced his side with a spear, and at once blood and water came out…These things occurred so that the scripture might be fulfilled, 'None of his bones shall be broken'" (John 19:34 and 36), which fulfilled the prophecy, again from today's psalm, "He will keep safe all his bones; not one of them shall be broken."

So what becomes of the brokenhearted? The Lord draws near to the broken hearted and gives unconditional love. Even if human love has departed, God's love has not departed—never has, never will.

And yes, "only love can break your heart," but in time the love of God heals it.

Today may the Holy Spirit draw near to the places in your heart that are broken, and minister anew God's healing love.

Amen.

The Gospel Is Not a Grand Illusion

They brought to [Jesus] a deaf man who had an impediment in his speech; and they begged him to lay hands on him. He took him aside in private, away from the crowd, and put his fingers into his ears, and he spat and touched his tongue. Then looking up to heaven, he sighed and said to him, "Ephphathah," that is, "Be opened." And immediately his ears were opened, his tongue was released, and he spoke plainly (Mark 7:32-35).

In the Name of the Father, Son, and Holy Spirit.

As human beings we all have a longing to be seen and heard for who we actually are. Ever since Facebook began in Mark Zuckerberg's dorm room at Harvard University in February 2004, online social media has mushroomed with many millions of people around the world spending time every day trying to be seen and heard. And yet, while on the surface social media has provided a means to be seen and heard, there is a dark underside.

Last year the American Psychiatric Association posted a fascinating article entitled, "Using Many Social Media Platforms Linked with Depression, Anxiety Risk" (January 17, 2017). This article asserts, "Research has suggested a link between spending extended time on social media and experiencing negative mental health outcomes" and that "the use of multiple social media platforms is strongly associated with depression and anxiety among young adults." Moreover, this study revealed that this depression and anxiety is magnified with the more social media platforms used. In other words, depression and anxiety are linked to using social media like Facebook—but when you are also juggling Twitter, Snapchat, Google Plus, Instagram, Pinterest, Reddit, Tumblr, LinkedIn, Vine, etc., that depression and anxiety can become even more pronounced.

Why? For one, the multitasking associated with keeping up with so many social media outlets simultaneously is a factor, as well the risk of committing a faux paus or gaffe (what is acceptable in one form of social media may not be in another). But there are deeper issues at play. One is the appearance that other people's lives are simply better than yours. On social media other people may seem happier and goofier than you, seem to have more friends and be better looking than you, seem to go on more exotic vacations and experience more academic or career success than you—and all this leads to an internal comparison vortex that will always leave you feeling somehow "less than" other people. And the longing to be seen and heard for who you actually are remains unfulfilled.

Back in the Stone Ages when I was a kid, many years before social media, when there were only four or five channels on television and the only way you knew what a band looked like was by the photographs on their album covers or in magazines like *Rolling Stone*, the classic rock band Styx sang this on the title track of their 1977 album *The Grand Illusion:*

> Don't be fooled by the radio
> The TV or the magazines
> They show you photographs of how your life should be
> But they're just someone else's fantasy
> So if you think your life is complete confusion
> Because you never win the game

> Just remember that it's a grand illusion
> And deep inside we're all the same

And while social media can be useful, often the images we project of ourselves in our attempt to be seen and heard are actually a "grand illusion" and incongruent with who we actually are, incongruent with the fact that yes, "deep inside we're all the same." In late 1999, just prior to the start of the new millennium, the award-winning author George Saunders stated this in an interview with CNN:

> Most of us spend our days the same way people spent their days in the year 1000: walking around smiling, trying to earn enough to eat, while neurotically doing these little self-proofs in our head about how much better we are than these other slobs, while simultaneously, in another part of our brain, secretly feeling woefully inadequate to these smarter, more beautiful people (*Gumption*, by Nick Offerman 302-303).

Can you relate?

Here is the good news…the gospel assures us that God sees and hears us as we actually are, not as we project ourselves to be on social media—and moreover, God loves us as we actually are, regardless of how we project ourselves to be. But we are dependent on God to open our eyes and ears to see and hear the gospel—as we pray for those who are being baptized, "Open their hearts to your grace and truth" (*BCP* 305). In other words we need God to open the eyes and ears of our heart to the reality of his unconditional love.

Along these lines I am going to juxtapose two illustrations—the first from one of the most influential women of the twentieth century, the second from one of the most influential rock albums ever.

A couple years ago in Tuscumbia, Alabama, I visited Ivy Green, the birthplace and childhood home of Helen Keller, who as you know was both deaf and blind. Helen was not born that way. As a toddler she had a horrific fever, and as her fever slowly faded away, so did her sight and hearing. Imagine not being able to see or hear anything. But one day at age six, Helen Keller's life suddenly took a new direction, as she wrote in her 1903 autobiography *The Story of My Life:*

> The most important day I remember in all my life is the one on which my teacher, Anne Mansfield Sullivan, came to me. I am filled with wonder when I consider the immeasurable contrasts between the two lives which it connects. It was the third of March 1887, three months before I was seven years old… "Light! Give me light!" was the wordless cry of my soul, and the light of love shone on me in that very hour. I felt approaching footsteps. I stretched out my hand as I supposed to my mother. Someone took it, and I was caught up and held close in the arms of her who had come to reveal all things to me, and, more than all things else, to love me (14-15).

Anne Sullivan and Helen Keller became lifelong friends. On the Ivy Green property there is the actual well where Anne taught Helen her first word: "water."

The second illustration…on their iconic 1969 double album entitled *Tommy* the British band The Who sang about a boy named Tommy, who like Helen Keller, was blind and deaf. Although as you may remember from their hit song "Pinball Wizard," that Tommy was a "deaf, dumb and blind kid (who) sure played a mean pinball," his inability to see, hear and speak left him feeling isolated—and there were some creepy characters who took advantage of him. On one of the shorter songs on the album, one of the characters calls out to Tommy:

> Tommy, can you hear me?
> Can you feel me near you?

> Tommy, can you see me?
> Can I help to cheer you?
> (From "Tommy Can You Hear Me?")

It is an upbeat little song, but the truth is Tommy cannot hear or see anyone or anything. Later on the album, Tommy utters a cry for help four times in a row: "See me, feel me, touch me, heal me—see me, feel me, touch me, heal me" (From "We're Not Gonna Take It/Listening to You"). But near the end of the album, Tommy finally experiences a breakthrough and sings:

> I'm free, I'm free
> And freedom tastes of reality
> I'm free, I'm free
> And I'm waiting for you to follow me
> (From "I'm Free")

If you have never listened to *Tommy* all the way through, trust me, it is an epic sonic experience. There is a reason it has been popular for nearly fifty years.

Metaphorically speaking, when it comes to the gospel, many of us are just like Helen Keller, just like Tommy—both blind and deaf. And in response to a blind and deaf world, God did not send a Facebook post or a Tweet, God sent his Son. To a blind world whose wordless cry echoed Helen Keller—"Light! Give me light!"—God sent Jesus, the Light of the World. To a deaf world God sent Jesus, the Word of God.

Many years before Jesus' incarnation the Old Testament prophet Isaiah prophesied in today's passage, "Here is your God. He will come and save you…the eyes of the blind shall be opened, and the ears of the deaf unstopped…then the tongue of the speechless (will) sing with joy" (Isaiah 35:4-6). Not only did Jesus in fact give sight to the blind (John 9:1-7), in today's gospel passage we see the literal fulfillment of Isaiah's prophecy about the deaf being healed as well:

> They brought to [Jesus] a deaf man who had an impediment in his speech; and they begged him to lay hands on him. He took him aside in private, away from the crowd, and put his fingers into his ears, and he spat and touched his tongue. Then looking up to heaven, he sighed and said to him, "Ephphathah," that is, "Be opened." And immediately his ears were opened, his tongue was released, and he spoke plainly (Mark 7:32-35).

Think about your life today. Is there a place in your heart where you feel lost in the dark and, like Helen Keller, are crying out, "Light! Give me light"? Or can you relate to Tommy's isolation and his cry, "see me, feel me, touch me, heal me"? Or maybe you have experienced some of the depression and anxiety linked to the use of multiple forms of social media because regardless of how you project your image to the world, you still feel isolated, like no one actually sees or hears you as you actually are.

But there is Someone who does…Jesus Christ, who not only sees and hears you as you actually are, but also loves you as you actually are, so much so that he died on the cross for you. Jesus sees right through all your social media images to your heart and offers you unconditional love. Scripture tells us that Jesus' death on the cross on Good Friday remains the definitive expression of God's unconditional love, that "God proves his love for us in that while we still were sinners Christ died for us" (Romans 5:8).

On Good Friday, the One who had opened the eyes of the blind was himself blindfolded by Roman soldiers and struck on his holy face. On Good Friday, the one who had spit and healed the deaf and mute man was himself spit on by his accusers and remained mute in response. On Good Friday, as Jesus died on the cross, Isaiah's prophecy, "Here is your God. He will come and save you" came to pass—and the light of love shone on a blind and deaf world "in that very hour."

Although the gospel is dismissed by some as a "grand illusion," it is in fact not an illusion at all, for that light of love still shines on the world, including you, even now.

Perhaps today God will open the eyes and ears of your heart to experience anew God's unconditional love—a love that, like Anne Sullivan showed to Helen Keller, can catch you up and hold you close, and pour out on you water of life from the Well of Life.

And who knows, you may even hear words from Jesus that echo Tommy: "I'm free, I'm free, and I'm waiting for you to follow me."

Amen.

The Inescapable Question

Jesus went on with his disciples to the villages of Caesarea Philippi; and on the way he asked his disciples, "Who do people say that I am?" And they answered him, "John the Baptist; and others, Elijah; and still others, one of the prophets." He asked them, "But who do you say that I am?" Peter answered him, "You are the Messiah." And he sternly ordered them not to tell anyone about him (Mark 8:27-30).

In the Name of the Father, Son, and Holy Spirit.

Throughout the past two millennia, there have been many theories about the identity of Jesus Christ. Debates about exactly who Jesus was and is continue to this day. Some believe Jesus is in fact what scripture asserts, the Son of God whose death and resurrection is the definitive expression of God's love. Others believe Jesus was not divine at all but rather a brilliant philosopher and teacher whose ethics, especially maxims like "Love your enemies" (Matthew 5:44), "Do to others as you would have them do to you" (Luke 6:31) and "Love your neighbor as yourself" (Matthew 22:39) would make the world a better place.

Others view Jesus as simply an influential religious figure akin to Abraham or Mohammad. Still others dismiss Jesus as a fraud or charlatan or imposter—as either completely misunderstood, or completely misguided.

Hollywood has portrayed Jesus in many ways as well, some favorably, some not so much. In the controversial 1999 film *Dogma*, George Carlin plays Cardinal Ignatius Glick, who, in an effort to make the Catholic Church more "hip" and "relatable," leads an effort called "Catholicism Wow!" He stands in front of a gothic church before an applauding audience and explains the new symbol of "Catholicism Wow":

> Now we all know how the majority and the media in this country view the Catholic Church. They think of us as a passé, archaic institution. People find the Bible obtuse, even hokey. Now in an effort to disprove all that, the church has appointed this year as a time of renewal both of faith and of style. For example, the crucifix, while it has been a time honored symbol of our faith, Holy Mother Church has decided to retire this highly recognizable yet wholly depressing image of our Lord crucified. Christ didn't come to earth to give us the willies. He came to help us out. He was a booster. And it's with that take on our Lord in mind that we have come up with a new more inspiring symbol.

A veiled statue is wheeled to the front—and Cardinal Glick continues, "So it is with great pleasure that I present you with the first of many revamps the "Catholicism Wow" campaign will unveil over the next year, I give you…the Buddy Christ!" The veil is taken off to reveal the Buddy Christ statue, which portrays Jesus with a huge grin on his face winking at you while pointing at you with his right hand and giving you a thumbs-up with his left hand. The crowd applauds its collective approval with oohs and aahs, and cameras flash. It is an absurd scene, and deeply offensive to some. While some interpret the scene as just plain blasphemous, I interpret it as a powerful statement about the danger of watering down the gospel, the danger of exchanging the truth about who Jesus actually is for something more palatable or relevant. Did Jesus, as Cardinal

Glick put it, simply come to "help us out" and be "a booster"—or is there more to it?

Scripture identifies Jesus in many ways: the Word (John 1:1), the Lamb of God who takes away the sin of the world (John 1:29), Emmanuel (Matthew 1:23), Prince of Peace (Isaiah 9:6), Friend of Sinners (Matthew 11:19), Head of the Church (Ephesians 4:15), Firstborn of all Creation (Colossians 1:15), Shepherd and Guardian of your souls (1 Peter 2:25), Alpha and Omega (Revelation 1:8), King of Kings and Lord of Lords (Revelation 19:16)—on and on it goes.

Jesus identified himself in many different ways: "I am the Bread of Life" (John 6:35), "I am the Light of the World" (John 8:12), "I am the Gate" (John 10:7), "I am the Good Shepherd" (John 10:11), "I am the Resurrection and the Life" (John 11:25), "I am the Way, the Truth and the Life" (John 14:6).

Scripture asserts that Jesus was both fully human, the Son of Man, and fully divine, the Son of God—that Jesus is Lord.

But in today's passage, Mark writes about Jesus asking his disciples one of the most important questions in all scripture, an inescapable question about who he is:

> Jesus went on with his disciples to the villages of Caesarea Philippi; and on the way he asked his disciples, "Who do people say that I am?" And they answered him, "John the Baptist; and others, Elijah; and still others, one of the prophets." He asked them, "But who do you say that I am?" Peter answered him, "You are the Messiah." And he sternly ordered them not to tell anyone about him (Mark 8:27-30).

Peter was right. Jesus is the Messiah, the Anointed One, the Savior of the world to whom the entire Old Testament, the Law and the Prophets, point. In Matthew's account of this episode, Peter's response to Jesus' question takes it a step further: "You are the Messiah, the Son of the living God" (Matthew 16:16).

And after Peter answered Jesus' question, "Who do you say that I am?" what did Jesus immediately begin teaching about his being the Messiah, the Son of God? Did he talk about being your Buddy Christ to help you out and be your booster? Did he talk about being the kind of Messiah that Israel, after many years of oppression at the hands of the Romans envisioned—a mighty military leader to lead a revolt against Rome? Not exactly. Mark continues, "Then [Jesus] began to teach them that the Son of Man must undergo great suffering, and be rejected by the elders, the chief priests, and the scribes, and be killed, and after three days rise again. He said this all quite openly" (Mark 8:31). In other words, Jesus began talking about his imminent death and resurrection.

Peter was emboldened by his correctly identifying Jesus as the Messiah, the Son of God, and "took [Jesus] aside and began to rebuke him" and was unpleasantly surprised to have Jesus in turn rebuke him, "Get behind me, Satan! For you are setting your mind not on divine things but on human things" (Mark 8:32-33).

Peter did not understand that Jesus, the Messiah, the Son of God, was born to die. It simply did not make any sense to him. And throughout the past two thousand years, this has not made sense to many people. This is nothing new. In his First Letter to the Corinthians, the Apostle Paul put it this way:

> The message about the cross is foolishness to those who are perishing, but to us who are being saved it is the power of God…Jews demand signs and Greeks desire wisdom, but we proclaim Christ crucified, a stumbling block to Jews and foolishness to Gentiles, but to those who are called, both Jews and Greeks, Christ the power of God and the wisdom of God. For God's foolishness is wiser than human wisdom, and God's weakness is stronger than human strength (1 Corinthians 1:18; 22-25).

Scripture always links who Jesus is—the Messiah, the Son of

God—with his death and resurrection. Jesus was and is much more than a wise philosopher or teacher, certainly much more than a Buddy Christ to help us out and be our booster.

During World War II, C. S. Lewis, who is best known for authoring the famous children's book series *The Chronicles of Narnia*, compiled a series of radio talks into his classic book, *Mere Christianity*. In this book C. S. Lewis makes his famous trilemma argument about Jesus being a Liar, a Lunatic, or the Lord:

> I am trying here to prevent anyone saying the really foolish thing that people often say about Him: "I'm ready to accept Jesus as a great moral teacher, but I don't accept His claim to be God." That is the one thing we must not say. A man who was merely a man and said the sort of things Jesus said would not be a great moral teacher. He would either be a lunatic—on a level with the man who says he is a poached egg—or else he would be the Devil of Hell. You must make your choice. Either this man was, and is, the Son of God: or else a madman or something worse. You can shut Him up for a fool, you can spit at Him and kill Him as a demon; or you can fall at His feet and call Him Lord and God. But let us not come with any patronizing nonsense about His being a great human teacher. He has not left that open to us. He did not intend to (*Mere Christianity* 40-41).

When it comes to Jesus being anyone other than Lord, C. S. Lewis would have none of it. If Jesus claimed to be the Son of God but knew he was not, he is a liar. If Jesus claimed to be the Son of God and really thought he was, but was not, he is a lunatic. If Jesus claimed to be the Son of God because he is, then he is Lord.

More recently biblical scholar Bart Ehrman has offered a fourth option to C. S. Lewis' trilemma, one that also begins with the letter L, asserting that Jesus' claim to be the Son of God is itself a Legend. But why would the apostles who were actual witnesses of the Risen Jesus suffer martyrdom for a legend? Wouldn't you think at least one of them in order to avoid a brutally painful death would have admitted that the idea of Jesus being the Messiah, the Son of God, was a hoax?

What did the Risen Jesus do for Thomas, who doubted his resurrection, who did not believe his fellow disciples who claimed they had seen him? Scripture tells us Jesus personally appeared again to his disciples, including Thomas, and said, "Peace be with you," and to Thomas directly, "Put your finger here and see my hands. Reach out your hand and put it in my side. Do not doubt but believe." And how did Thomas respond? "My Lord and my God" (John 20:26-28).

The Risen Jesus pointed Thomas to his scars, scars that attest to the good news of the gospel that God's love for Thomas, God's love for the world, God's love for you, is a love so great that he willingly died on the cross for all of us. And Thomas responded exactly how C. S. Lewis wrote, falling at his feet and calling Jesus, "My Lord and my God." Can there be any other appropriate response?

This personal response to the love of God is mirrored by Paul as he wrote to the Galatians, "The life I now live in the flesh I live by faith in the Son of God, who loved me and gave himself for me" (Galatians 2:20).

But enough about Cardinal Glick, and Peter, and C. S. Lewis and Bart Ehrman, and Thomas, and Paul…what about you? The same inescapable question Jesus asked his disciples at Caesarea Philippi he asks you today: "Who do you say that I am?"

Remember what Jesus did after Peter correctly answered his question? Mark tells us, "[Jesus] sternly ordered them not to tell anyone about him." This is known as the Messianic Secret, that during his earthly ministry, Jesus, even after performing miracles, did not want his identity as the Messiah, the Son of God, revealed yet.

Why? Because Jesus himself would fully reveal his identity as the Messiah, the Son of God, on Good Friday and Easter Sunday.

When Jesus died, Mark tells us that the Roman centurion who stood guard at the cross turned to face him when he drew his last breath and then proclaimed, "Truly this man was God's son!" (Mark 15:39). Moreover, scripture tells us that Jesus "was declared to be Son of God with power according to the spirit of holiness by resurrection from the dead" (Romans 1:4). The death and resurrection of Jesus, the Messiah, the Son of God, means the Messianic Secret was no longer a secret.

The good news of the gospel is that Jesus is who he claimed to be, the Son of God, and that this same Jesus indeed loved you and gave himself for you, and he still bears the scars from that. The unconditional love of God for you is no secret at all.

Today, may the Holy Spirit quicken your heart to respond to Jesus' inescapable question—"Who do you say that I am?"—like Peter and Thomas, "You are the Messiah, the Son of God…my Lord and my God."

Amen.

The Powerful Mercy of God

If any of you put a stumbling block before one of these little ones who believe in me, it would be better for you if a great millstone were hung around your neck and you were thrown into the sea. If your hand causes you to stumble, cut it off; it is better for you to enter life maimed than to have two hands and to go to hell, to the unquenchable fire. And if your foot causes you to stumble, cut it off; it is better for you to enter life lame than to have two feet and to be thrown into hell. And if your eye causes you to stumble, tear it out; it is better for you to enter the kingdom of God with one eye than to have two eyes and to be thrown into hell, where their worm never dies, and the fire is never quenched (Mark 9:42-48).

In the Name of the Father, Son, and Holy Spirit.

As you know we talk a lot about God's grace here at Christ Church because God's grace is at the heart of the gospel. Today though, I am preaching on God's mercy, which is connected to God's grace but not the same thing. Metaphorically God's grace and mercy are two sides of the same coin. Grace is God giving us what we do not deserve, unconditional love. Mercy is God not giving us what we do deserve, punishment for our sins.

In today's gospel passage Jesus minces no words in making it crystal clear that all of us, no exceptions, are in need of God's mercy:

> If any of you put a stumbling block before one of these little ones who believe in me, it would be better for you if a great millstone were hung around your neck and you were thrown into the sea. If your hand causes you to stumble, cut it off; it is better for you to enter life maimed than to have two hands and to go to hell, to the unquenchable fire. And if your foot causes you to stumble, cut it off; it is better for you to enter life lame than to have two feet and to be thrown into hell. And if your eye causes you to stumble, tear it out; it is better for you to enter the kingdom of God with one eye than to have two eyes and to be thrown into hell, where their worm never dies, and the fire is never quenched (Mark 9:42-48).

This is without question one of the most sobering passages in scripture. It is not a passage about which will see inspirational Christian calendars or mugs, not a passage about which a Vacation Bible School curriculum will be developed (the crafts for that would be "interesting"). And yet Jesus himself said it—so if you have a "red letter" edition of the Bible like I do, these words are all in red—there is no skirting around them. This passage is sobering because it describes what all of us have done at one time or another. Have you never caused someone else to stumble? Have you never sinned with your hands or sprinted after temptation on your feet? Have your eyes never caused you to sin?

In this passage Jesus does what he so often did in his preaching and teaching—he goes straight to the heart. Similarly in his Sermon on the Mount Jesus warns:

> You have heard it said to those of ancient times, "You shall not murder"; and "whoever murders shall be liable to judgment." But I say to you that if you are angry with a brother or sister, you will be liable to judgment; and if you insult a brother or sister, you will be liable to the council; and if you say, "You fool," you will be liable to the hell of fire (Matthew 5:21-22).

And it gets worse, as Jesus continues:

> You have heard that it was said, "You shall not commit adultery." But I say to you that everyone who looks at a woman with lust has already committed adultery with her in his heart. If your right eye causes you to sin, tear it out and throw it away; it is better for you to lose one of your members than for your whole body to be thrown into hell. And if your right hand causes you to sin, cut it off and throw it away; it is better for you to lose one of your members than for your whole body to go into hell (Matthew 5:27-30)

And yes, every word of Jesus' Sermon on the Mount is also red in the "red letter" editions of the Bible.

So what do we do with all this? After all, Jesus does not mitigate the requirements of God's holy law; he turns up the heat even more. In these passages Jesus shows all of us, no exceptions, what we need so desperately from God: mercy. And that, thankfully, is where the gospel comes in.

In the same way the gospel passage appointed for today is one of the most sobering in scripture, the collect appointed for today is one of the most comforting: "O God, you declare your almighty power chiefly in showing mercy and pity: Grant us the fullness of your grace" (*BCP* 234). Again, in this collect, we see that God's grace and mercy are two sides of the same coin. The gospel is very good news for sinners like you and me because the gospel contains not only the fullness of God's grace, but also demonstrates that God shows his "almighty power chiefly in showing mercy."

In his hit 1986 album entitled *So* Peter Gabriel sings a hauntingly beautiful song called "Mercy Street" in which he writes about the mercy we all need:

> Confessing all the secret things in the warm velvet box
> To the priest, he's the doctor

> He can handle the shocks...
> Dreaming of Mercy Street
> Where you're inside out
> Dreaming of mercy in your daddy's arms again
> Dreaming of Mercy Street
> I swear they moved that sign
> Looking for mercy in your daddy's arms
> Mercy, mercy, looking for mercy
> Mercy, mercy, looking for mercy
> Looking for mercy

At a 2003 live performance of this song in Milan, Italy, Peter Gabriel simply walked around in a slow circle whispering, "Mercy, looking for mercy...mercy, looking for mercy." Peter Gabriel is not alone. In our own way, each of us is also walking in circles looking for mercy.

Let me share an example of a time I experienced mercy many years ago, which of course, is much less embarrassing than a more recent example would be. When I was in middle school I went on a camp weekend with a bunch of friends. We spent most of the time outside playing sports, enjoying the campfires, reveling in the amazing May weather. We stayed in cabins that weekend, and those of us in our cabin thought it would be fun to sneak out that Saturday night and run around the camp like hooligans because, well, we were middle schoolers. The chaperones heard about this and as a preemptive strike one of them literally placed his bed against the door of the cabin.

However, around 2:30 that morning, several of us gathered around the sleeping chaperone and quietly and gently lifted his bed and moved it away from the door, and then sprinted outside and began running around the camp and yelling like banshees. Needless to say the next morning we were all read the Riot Act. Later that day when our parents came to pick us up my dad walked over to the same chaperone we had "moved out of our way." I tried to cut dad off at the pass. "Hey dad! I'm ready to go!" and tried to steer him back to the car, but it was too late. "Hope my son behaved himself," my dad said to the chaperone.

I waited for the ax to fall, but to my shock, the chaperone smiled and patted me on the back. "Dave's a great kid," he said; "we all had a really fun weekend." Then he turned and began greeting other parents while my dad and I walked to the car. I was stunned. The next time I saw that chaperone I thanked him and he grinned, "I don't know what you're talking about" with a gleam in his eye that said, "I know exactly what you're talking about, but it's okay." That is what mercy looks like. Did the chaperone's mercy cause me to act like a hooligan on the next camping trip? No, it had the exact opposite effect. From then on, I treated that merciful chaperone with the utmost respect. The mercy that chaperone showed me mirrors the gospel, that God indeed shows his almighty power "chiefly in showing mercy."

Scripture shows this again and again. In Exodus we read the account of God passing by in front of Moses and proclaiming, "The Lord, the Lord, a God merciful and gracious, slow to anger, and abounding in steadfast love and faithfulness" (Exodus 34:6). In Psalm 136 the psalmist begins, "Give thanks to the Lord, for he is good, for his mercy endures forever," and in case you missed it the first time, repeats the refrain "his mercy endures forever" twenty-five more times in that psalm: "his mercy endures forever… his mercy endures forever…his mercy endures forever"…on and on it goes.

In his Letter to the Romans the Apostle Paul emphasizes that for both Jews and Gentiles, the mercy of God has the last word:

> The gifts and the calling of God are irrevocable. Just as you were once disobedient to God but now have received mercy because of their disobedience, so they have now been disobedient in order that, by the mercy shown to you, they too may now receive mercy. For God has imprisoned all in disobedience so that he

may be merciful to all. O the depth of the riches and wisdom and knowledge of God! (Romans 11:29-33).

Scripture also tells us God is "rich in mercy" (Ephesians 2:4), that "mercy triumphs over judgment" (James 2:13). God's mercy is the central theme of the Prayer of Humble Access, "We do not presume to come to this thy Table, O *merciful* Lord, trusting in our own righteousness, but in thy manifold and great *mercies*... thou art the same Lord whose property is always to have *mercy*" (*BCP* 337). Each week we begin our confession: "Most *merciful* God..." (*BCP* 360).

The ultimate expression of the mercy of God, of God not giving us what we deserve, occurred on Good Friday, when God in Christ, took the punishment for our sins upon himself, when Jesus was shown no mercy at all.

Although Jesus' eyes were not plucked out, they were blackened by the blows of the soldiers—and although his hands and feet were not cut off, they were shattered as large nails were driven through them into the wood of the cross. Metaphorically, the millstone that should have been tied around our necks before being tossed into the sea was tied around Jesus' neck instead as he died in our place and, as the Old Testament prophet Micah foretold, "cast all our sins into the depth of the sea" (Micha 7:19). And before being raised from the dead, as we state in The Apostles' Creed, Jesus "descended into hell."

In other words, the road Jesus walked to Calvary, the Via Dolorosa, could also be called Mercy Street. On the cross Jesus showed the fullness of God's grace and God's almighty power chiefly in showing mercy, mercy God continues to show even now. If that were not true, none of us would be here. How do we respond to the powerful mercy of God? Jesus tells exactly what to do:

> Two men went up to the temple to pray, one a Pharisee and the other a tax collector. The Pharisee,

standing by himself, was praying thus, "God, I thank you that I am not like other people: thieves, rogues, adulterers, or even like this tax collector. I fast twice a week; I give a tenth of all my income." But the tax collector, standing far off, would not even look up to heaven, but was beating his breast and saying, "God, be merciful to me, a sinner!" [Jesus concludes] I tell you, this man went down to his home justified rather than the other (Luke 18:10-14).

In other words, we ask for God's mercy, we receive God's mercy…and we share it with others—"Blessed are the merciful, for they will receive mercy" (Matthew 5:7)…"Be merciful, just as your [Heavenly] Father is merciful" (Luke 6:36).

The gospel is good news for all those walking in circles looking for mercy, because God indeed shows his almighty power "chiefly in showing mercy" and assures you that one day in heaven you too will receive "mercy in your daddy's arms."

Amen.

Grace? Grace.

For by a single offering [Jesus] has perfected for all time those who are sanctified. And the Holy Spirit also testifies to us, for after saying, "This is the covenant that I will make with them after those days, says the Lord: I will put my laws in their hearts, and I will write them on their minds," he also adds, "I will remember their sins and their lawless deeds no more." Where there is forgiveness of these, there is no longer any offering for sin (Hebrews 10:14-18).

In the Name of the Father, Son, and Holy Spirit.

The bestselling author Mitch Albom recently finished his most recent book, *The Next Person You Meet in Heaven* (2018). The premise of this book, like its prequel, *The Five People You Meet in Heaven* (2003), is that in heaven you meet five different people who predeceased you and who had a major impact on your life, even if you were unaware of it, and who teach you something specific that gives you clearer perspective on what happened during your earthly life.

In *The Next Person You Meet in Heaven*, the protagonist is Annie, a newlywed who on the day after her wedding was on a hot air balloon ride with her new husband Paulo. They collided with some powerlines, and her husband died, but she survived. However, Annie had a near-death experience during which she met her mom Lorraine in heaven.

Annie's father had left her and Lorraine when Annie was a little girl. One evening, Lorraine and her boyfriend took Annie to an amusement park called Ruby Pier and left Annie to fend for herself. But there was a tragic accident that resulted in Annie having her left hand severed. Although her hand was surgically reattached, she was very embarrassed by the scars, and always wore long sleeved shirts even in summer to keep her scars covered.

After Annie's accident, her mother Lorraine was wracked with guilt for not being there to keep Annie from getting hurt. From then on, she overcompensated and became a suffocating overprotective mother, and this resulted in Annie deeply resenting her and leaving home after her high school graduation. When Annie finally reconnected with her mother, she was dying of cancer. Lorraine died before she and Annie were fully reconciled, which unfortunately is not uncommon in families. This time, Annie was the one wracked with guilt.

But during her near-death experience Annie meets her mom in heaven, and something very significant happens. Mitch Albom writes:

> In the blue river of the afterlife, Lorraine cupped her hands and lifted water up, watching it pour through her fingers. "This is your heaven?" Annie asked. "Isn't it beautiful? I wanted serenity after all the conflict of my life. Here I enjoy a calm I never knew on earth." "And you've been waiting for me all this time?" "What's time between a mother and her daughter? Never too much, never enough." "Mom?" "Yes." "We fought a lot." "I know." She took Annie's left hand and guided it into the water. "But is that all you remember?"
>
> Annie felt her fingers floating and her mind doing the same. In the water's reflection she saw only loving scenes from her childhood, countless memories,

her mother kissing her goodnight, unwrapping a new toy, plopping whipped cream onto pancakes, putting Annie on her first bicycle, stitching a ripped dress, sharing a tube of lipstick, pushing a button to Annie's favorite radio station. It was as if someone unlocked a vault and all these fond recollections could be examined at once.

"Why didn't I feel this before?" she whispered. "Because we embrace our scars more than our healing," Lorraine said. "We can recall the exact day we got hurt, but who remembers the day the wound was gone? From the moment you woke up in that hospital, I was different with you, and you were different with me. You were sullen. You were mad. You fought with me constantly. You hated my restrictions. But that wasn't the real reason for your anger, was it?"

Lorraine reached down and clutched Annie's fingers. "Can you break that last secret? Can you say the real reason for your resentment since Ruby Pier?" Annie choked up. Her voice was barely a whisper. "Because you weren't there to save me." Lorraine closed her eyes. "That's right. Can you forgive me for that?" "Mom." "Yes?" "You don't need to hear me say it." "No, I don't," Lorraine said softly. "But you do."

Annie began to cry again, tears of release, blessed release, the expulsion of secrets bottled up for years. She realized the sacrifices Lorraine had made before and after that day at Ruby Pier… She thought about her mother's small funeral, and how much of Lorraine's life had been surrendered to protect Annie's. "Yes, yes, I forgive you, Mom. Of course I forgive you. I didn't know. I love you." Lorraine placed her hands together. "Grace?" "Grace." "*That*," Lorraine said, smiling, "is what I was here to teach you" (148-150).

As you know, we talk a lot about grace here at Christ Church, because grace, God's one-way unconditional love in Jesus Christ, is the heart of the gospel. Moreover, grace is directly connected with forgiveness, which is not only the central theme of the passage I just read, but is also the central theme in today's New Testament passage from the Letter to the Hebrews. In this passage the writer refers back to an Old Testament prophesy from Jeremiah (31:33-34) and underscores the central place of forgiveness in the gospel:

> For by a single offering [Jesus] has perfected for all time those who are sanctified. And the Holy Spirit also testifies to us, for after saying "This is the covenant that I will make with them after those days, says the Lord: I will put my laws in their hearts, and I will write them on their minds," he also adds, "I will remember their sins and their lawless deeds no more." Where there is forgiveness of these, there is no longer any offering for sin (Hebrews 10:14-18).

According to this passage, Jesus' death on the cross, Jesus' "single offering" of himself means you are forgiven by God, and that "where there is forgiveness…there is no longer any offering for sin." Do you believe that?

Forgiveness was at the heart of Jesus' earthly ministry. One of the earlier miracles Jesus performed involved a paralytic whose friends carried him to a house where Jesus was healing people. They could not get to Jesus through the boisterous crowd, so they carried their friend up onto the top of the roof, broke a hole in the roof and lowered him down to Jesus. When Jesus saw this, what was the first thing he said? Jesus looked at the paralytic and gently said, "Son, your sins are forgiven" (Mark 2:5). Of course Jesus also healed him physically, as he later said to him, "Stand up, take your mat and go home" (Mark 2:11). The paralytic had not asked for forgiveness, but apparently from Jesus' perspective it was more important that the paralytic knew he was forgiven than it was to walk.

And it is the same with you.

Later in his earthly ministry Jesus was at a house party that a Pharisee was hosting. Many of the guests were the wealthy movers and shakers of the community, the "town and gown" set. During the meal a prostitute who had experienced God's forgiveness through Jesus' ministry walked right up to Jesus in the middle of this party and started weeping and bathing Jesus' feet with her tears. Then she took the most valuable possession she had, an alabaster jar of perfume, and broke it open and poured it out on Jesus' feet. The others there were indignant, in disbelief about her audacity. But Jesus said, "I tell you, her sins, which were many, have been forgiven." Then in the same way Jesus had done with the paralytic, he looked at her and said, "Your sins are forgiven… go in peace" (Luke 7:36-50).

Again, it is the same with you. Your sins are forgiven.

I suspect some of you still doubt that you are forgiven by God. Perhaps you think God is still keeping score on your life, meticulously recording in his book every time you mess up in one way or another. But because of Jesus' "single offering" on the cross, because "there is no longer any offering for sin," scripture assures you that God has forgiven you, that in Jesus you "have redemption through his blood, the forgiveness of [your] trespasses according to the riches of his grace that he lavished on [you]" (Ephesians 1:7-8). Grace? Grace.

In response to God's forgiveness, we are called to forgive others. This is probably not a new concept for you, but it something of which we all need to be reminded. "Be kind to one another, tenderhearted," scripture tells us, "forgiving one another as God in Christ has forgiven you" (Ephesians 4:32).

There is one more aspect to this forgiveness. Back to Mitch Albom for a moment…his first and most famous book is *Tuesdays with Morrie*, which recounts conversations he had with Morrie Schwartz, a sociology professor who had impacted his life many years before. Morrie was dying, and so for fourteen straight weeks on Tuesday morning Mitch flew from his home in Michigan to New England, visited with Morrie that afternoon, and then flew back to Michigan that night. Here's what Morrie told Mitch on the twelfth Tuesday: "Forgive yourself before you die. Then forgive others… There is no point in keeping vengeance or stubbornness. These things"—he sighed—"these things I so regret in my life. Pride. Vanity. Why do we do the things we do?" (164). Morrie continues:

> "It's not just other people we need to forgive, Mitch. We also need to forgive ourselves." Ourselves? "Yes. For all the things we didn't do. All the things we should have done. You can't get stuck on the regrets of what should have happened. That doesn't help you when you get to where I am. I always wished I had done more with my work; I wished I had written more books. I used to beat myself up over it. Now I see that never did any good. Make peace. You need to make peace with yourself and everyone around you… Forgive yourself. Forgive others. Don't wait, Mitch. Not everyone gets the time I'm getting. Not everyone is as lucky" (166-167).

On Good Friday, Jesus died to atone for your sins, to ensure that you are forgiven, completely—no exceptions, no qualifications, no disclaimers. Right after being nailed to the cross, Jesus prayed for forgiveness for the world and for you, "Father, forgive them, for they do not know what they are doing" (Luke 23:34). When it comes to sin and forgiveness, we often do not know what we are doing…but God does, and God has chosen to forgive.

Maybe, like Annie in *The Next Person You Meet in Heaven*, there was a time in your life when you got really hurt, and there was not someone there to save you. If so, chances are you remember the exact day you got hurt. And perhaps like Annie you are ashamed of the scars that wound left you, and you are always wearing metaphorical long sleeve shirts to keep those scars hidden, even in the summer.

What you do with your scars is up to you, but the Risen Jesus has never tried to hide his scars from Good Friday, his scars from the exact day he got hurt and was wounded for your transgressions. In addition to the other people you will meet in heaven someday, you will meet the One who died to save you.

"By a single offering [Jesus] has perfected for all time those who are sanctified…there is no longer any offering for sin."

Jesus' words to the paralytic and the prostitute are his words to you: "Your sins are forgiven." That is the good news of the gospel.

Grace? Grace.

Amen.

Your Redemption Is Drawing Near

There will be signs in the sun, the moon, and the stars, and on the earth distress among nations confused by the roaring of the sea and the waves. People will faint from fear and foreboding of what is coming upon the world, for the powers of the heavens will be shaken. Then they will see 'the Son of Man coming in a cloud' with power and great glory. Now when these things begin to take place, stand up and raise your heads, because your redemption is drawing near (Luke 21:25-28).

In the Name of the Father, Son, and Holy Spirit.

Today is the First Sunday of Advent, the beginning of a new church year. Ironically the new church year begins as the calendar year ends, as in the northern hemisphere the daylight lessens and there a little more darkness each day. But with the grace of God, when it looks like things are coming to an end, things are just getting started.

The word Advent means "arrival." During Advent we wear metaphorical bifocals as we anticipate celebrating anew Jesus' first arrival at his incarnation and anticipate his next arrival, the Second Coming, when as we pray in *The Book of Common Prayer* Jesus will return "in glorious majesty" (395).

I am sucker for sentimental Christmas movies. My favorite

movie of all time is now and will forever be the 1946 classic *It's a Wonderful Life*. I recently watched a much more recent film, the British romantic comedy, *Love Actually*, which was made the year after the tragedy of 9/11. The opening scene caught me off guard and made me tear up. It is a montage of people greeting and embracing one another at Heathrow Airport in London—image after image of hugs and smiles and kisses, image after image of people being welcomed by their loved ones. During this sequence one of the film's ensemble cast, Hugh Grant, narrates in a voiceover:

> Whenever I get gloomy with the state of the world, I think about the arrivals gate at Heathrow Airport. General opinion's starting to make out that we live in a world of hatred and greed, but I don't see that. It seems to me that love is everywhere. Often, it's not particularly dignified or newsworthy, but it's always there—fathers and sons, mothers and daughters, husbands and wives, boyfriends, girlfriends, old friends. When the planes hit the Twin Towers, as far as I know, none of the phone calls from the people on board were messages of hate or revenge—they were all messages of love. If you look for it, I've got a sneaky feeling you'll find that love actually is all around.

There are many people who as Hugh Grant said, are "gloomy with the state of the world." We live in a time of great anxiety, increasing climate change, bitter political polarization, one mass shooting after another—in a time in which we see again and again that racism, sexism, antisemitism, corruption are all alive and well. And we do not need a motivational speech or a self-help strategy or someone else to blame—we need the grace of God, we need to be reminded that indeed "love actually is all around."

The setting of today's gospel passage is Holy Week, as Jesus' earthly life and ministry were coming to end, as metaphorically there was a little more darkness each day. As the darkness of Good Friday loomed ever nearer Jesus taught about his Second Coming, which will be during a dark time when it looks like things are coming to an end. Jesus warned, "There will be signs in the sun, the moon, and the stars, and on the earth distress among nations confused by the roaring of the sea and the waves. People will faint from fear and foreboding of what is coming upon the world, for the powers of the heavens will be shaken" (Luke 21:25-26).

But Jesus continued with words of hope, "Then they will see 'the Son of Man coming in a cloud' with power and great glory. Now when these things begin to take place, stand up and raise your heads, because your redemption is drawing near" (Luke 21:27-28). When things look the darkest, like they are coming to an end, the grace of God is just getting started. Your redemption is drawing near.

One of the recurring themes in the scriptures appointed for Advent is the theme of light coming into darkness, the light of God's grace coming into the darkness of our lives. Many of us as children were afraid of the dark. When I was young, at night I was convinced that monsters lurked under my bed or in my closet. As we get older we may still find ourselves afraid of the dark. In his epic masterpiece, *Les Misérables*, Victor Hugo ominously describes why we are afraid of the dark:

> Darkness is dizzying. We need light; whenever we plunge into the opposite of day we feel our hearts chilled. When the eye sees darkness, the mind sees trouble. In an eclipse, at night, in the sooty darkness, even the strongest feel anxiety. Nobody walks alone at night in the forest without trembling. Darkness and trees, two formidable depths—a chimeric reality appears in the indistinct distance...You breathe in the odors of the great black void.

He continues:

> You are afraid and are tempted to look behind you. The socket of night, the haggard look of everything,

taciturn profiles that fade away as you advance, obscure dishevelments, angry clumps, livid pools, the gloomy reflected in the funereal, the sepulchral immensity of silence, the possible unknown beings, swaying of mysterious branches, frightful torsos of the tress, long wisps of shivering grass—you are defenseless against all of it (Signet Classics edition 386).

Hugo then adds, "This penetration of the darkness is inexpressibly sinister for a child" (386). Perhaps you can remember specific times you were afraid of the dark as a child. In some way you may be afraid of the dark right now.

And yet the grace of God often encounters us unexpectedly when we are the most afraid of the dark. At the beginning of her recently published memoir entitled *In Pieces*, Sally Field, the iconic multiple Oscar and Emmy winning actress, describes a powerful moment when she experienced grace as a child in the dark:

> In the eighth grade…I had my first performance night in the school auditorium. For the first time I walked on a stage in front of an audience of parents and friends, there to watch, among other things, my Juliet—not the whole play, just two scenes: the potion scene and the death scene. My mother drove me home afterward, and I clearly remember sitting in that dark car beside her. I desperately wanted to know what she thought but was afraid to ask, so I just watched her drive. Sometimes the headlights of an oncoming car would light up the whole interior, making it seem even darker after it passed. But when her face was bright with light she looked at me, and as if we were hiding from someone, she whispered, "You were magical." I whispered back, "I was?" Then everything was dark again and I could barely see her at all. "What does that mean?" I asked. "Just that." Another flash of headlights lit up the front seat and I could see her mouth edging toward a smile, the light

bleaching her beautiful face white, then slowly fading to black (2-3).

Victor Hugo was right, "Darkness is dizzying. We need light... When the eye sees darkness, the mind sees trouble." That is when the grace of God meets us.

And that grace of God that meets us unexpectedly in the dark is often episodic, just like Sally Field recalled about that car ride in the dark with her mom. We get a brief glimpse of the beautiful grace of God that is always with us, even when and especially when we are afraid of the dark—and we are reminded "that love is actually all around." Scripture assures us that in the same way the young Sally Field got a brief glimpse of grace in the light shining on the face of her mom in the car that night, God meets us in the dark with his beautiful grace in the face of Jesus Christ—as Paul wrote to the Corinthians, "It is God who said, 'Let light shine out of darkness,' who has shone in our hearts to give the light of the knowledge of the glory of God in the face of Jesus Christ" (2 Corinthians 4:6).

Jesus, who just prior to healing a man blind from birth identified himself as "the light of the world" (John 8:12) arrived in a dark world in the middle of a dark night. A few months before Jesus' birth in Bethlehem his cousin, John the Baptist was born. And that is when John the Baptist's father Zechariah, prophesied, "By the tender mercy of our God, the dawn from on high will break upon us, to give light to those who sit in darkness and in the shadow of death" (Luke 1:78-79).

A few days after Jesus proclaimed, "Stand up and raise your heads, because your redemption is drawing near," things grew darker and darker all the way to Good Friday. On Good Friday what Victor Hugo identified as "Darkness and trees, two formidable depths" met as Jesus, suffered on the tree of life, the cross. And when Jesus was nailed to the cross he did not send messages of hate or revenge, but a message of love, "Father, forgive them; for they do not know what they are doing" (Luke 23:34). On the cross "the tender mercy of our God, the dawn from on high" indeed broke upon the dark world.

Jesus' unconditional love given in his death on the cross was "not particularly dignified" but it certainly was and certainly is newsworthy, good news worthy, gospel worthy—for it the definitive expression of God's unexpected grace given to a world afraid of the dark. As Jesus was crucified scripture tells us, "From noon on, darkness came over the whole land until three in the afternoon"—or as the great seventeenth century Anglican priest and poet John Donne (1572-1631) put it in the very last sermon he ever preached, on the cross "those glorious eyes grew faint in their light: so as the Sun ashamed to survive them, departed with his light too" (*The Sermons of John Donne, Volume X*, 247-248).

Jesus died in the dark, followed by "the sepulchral immensity of silence." But God was not done shining grace into a dark world, not at all, for as scripture also tells us, "The light shines in the darkness, and the darkness did not overcome it" (John 1:5). Early on Easter morning, when it was darkest just before the dawn, Jesus rose from the grave, and showed the grace of God in his beautiful face to world still afraid of the dark. When it looked like things were coming to an end, the grace of God was just getting started.

Back to *Les Misérables* for a moment…the reason Victor Hugo was describing in such depth the horror of being alone in the dark, especially for a child, was because at that point in the novel the little child Cossette was alone in the dark woods. She had been sent by her abusive "caretakers" to get a large pail of water in the middle of the night. But as she struggled to carry this heavy pail of water back through the dark woods, Cossette was given unexpected grace—as Hugo writes:

> She was worn out and was not yet out of the forest.

> Reaching an old chestnut tree she knew, she made one last halt, longer than the others, to rest up well; then she gathered all her strength, took up the bucket again, and began to walk on courageously. Meanwhile the poor little despairing thing could not help crying: "Oh my God! Oh God!"
>
> At that moment she suddenly felt that the weight of the bucket was gone. A hand, which seemed enormous to her, had just caught the handle, and was carrying it easily. She looked up…A man who had come up behind her and whom she had not heard. This man, without saying a word, had grasped the handle of the bucket she was carrying. There are instincts for all the crises of life. The child was not afraid (387).

When Cossette was alone and afraid in the dark, reaching the end of her strength, she unexpectedly experienced grace from Jean Valjean, grace that was just getting started, grace that would transform her life.

The gospel is good news for a world afraid of the dark, for indeed "love actually is all around." And Jesus' words during Holy Week are his words to you today: "Stand up and raise your heads, because your redemption is drawing near."

Amen.

Grace for Those Drifting Too Far from the Shore

In the fifteenth year of the reign of Emperor Tiberius, when Pontius Pilate was governor of Judea, and Herod was ruler of Galilee, and his brother Philip ruler of the region of Ituraea and Trachonitis, and Lysanias ruler of Abilene, during the high priesthood of Annas and Caiaphas, the word of God came to John son of Zechariah in the wilderness. He went into all the region around the Jordan, proclaiming a baptism of repentance for the forgiveness of sins, as it is written in the book of the words of the prophet Isaiah, "The voice of one crying out in the wilderness: 'Prepare the way of the Lord, make his paths straight. Every valley shall be filled, and every mountain and hill shall be made low, and the crooked shall be made straight, and the rough ways made smooth; and all flesh shall see the salvation of God'" (Luke 3:1-6).

In the Name of the Father, Son, and Holy Spirit.

I recently watched Martin Scorsese's brilliant 2005 documentary, *No Direction Home*, about the early career of Bob Dylan. Near the beginning of this film Bob Dylan recollects that when he was a young boy he and his family moved into a house in the obscure small town of Hibbing, Minnesota. Specifically they moved to 2425 Seventh Avenue East, if you were wondering. Why would

I know that? Glad you asked! Several summers ago I was driving from North Dakota, across Minnesota, to Wisconsin and visited Hibbing on the way, where I talked with a longtime bartender who was a childhood friend of Bob Dylan. He told me exactly where the house was, and that the current owners were really nice. So I went to the house and rang the doorbell…but alas, there was nobody home. At least I got to stand on the front step and ring the doorbell.

The previous occupants of this house had left behind several pieces of furniture, including an old mahogany turntable that played 78 rpm records. In fact, there was a record still on it. The young Bob Dylan—who at that point still went by his birth name, Robert Zimmerman—played it and heard a song written by a Georgia-born gospel songwriter named Charles Moody (1894-1950), a song called "Drifting Too Far from the Shore" recorded by The New Lost City Ramblers, who sang:

> Out on the perilous deep
> Where dangers silently creep
> And storms so violently sweep
> You are drifting too far from the shore
> Drifting too far from the shore
> You are drifting too far from the shore
> Come to Jesus today
> Let him show you the way
> You are drifting too far from the shore

And that was the moment music grabbed ahold of Bob Dylan.

"Drifting too far from the shore…you are drifting too far from the shore"…all of us, if we are honest, know exactly what that feels like. But the good news of the gospel is that even if we find ourselves drifting too far from the shore, it is never too far for the grace of God. In Psalm 139, the psalmist wrote:

> Where can I go from your Spirit? Where can I flee
> from your presence? If I climb up to heaven, you are

there; if I make the grave my bed, you are there also. If I take the wings of the morning and dwell in the uttermost parts of the sea, even there your hand will lead me and your right hand hold me fast (Psalm 13:6-9, *BCP* 794).

Yet when we are drifting too far from the shore, we can feel very disoriented, very lost. In the 1990 film *Quigley Down Under*, Tom Selleck plays Matthew Quigley, an American sharp shooter from the Old West. By the way, my grandmother had a Tom Selleck poster in her house, which made me a little uncomfortable, but that is another sermon for another time.

Matthew Quigley answers an advertisement from a man named Elliot Marston in Australia seeking someone with his skill set, but when he arrives he learns he is wanted in order to eradicate the Aborigines. He refuses, and is then beaten and left for dead in the Australian outback, along with a woman known as Crazy Cora. Matthew Quigley and Crazy Cora later have the following conversation:

> Crazy Cora begins, "You know, if we're lost, you can tell me." Quigley is blunt: "We're lost." Crazy Cora continues, "I can take bad news, just tell me straight," and Quigley replies, "I don't know where the heck we are." Crazy Cora presses, "No sense taking time to make it sound better than it is." Quigley says, "I reckon we're going in circles." Crazy Cora persists, "Wire things up and I'll see right through, so just tell me honestly, are we lost?" Quigley takes a different tack: "Nope, I know exactly where we are." Crazy Cora: "That's good, 'cause frankly I was getting a little worried."

In today's passage we see that when we are lost in the wilderness, when we are drifting too far from the shore, that the grace of God still meets us. Luke writes about John the Baptist being the "voice in the wilderness" God had sent to call people to repentance. Luke does not write, "once upon a time," because the gospel is not a fairy tale. Rather, Luke anchors this event in history:

> In the fifteenth year of the reign of Emperor Tiberius, when Pontius Pilate was governor of Judea, and Herod was ruler of Galilee, and his brother Philip ruler of the region of Ituraea and Trachonitis, and Lysanias ruler of Abilene, during the high priesthood of Annas and Caiaphas, the word of God came to John son of Zechariah in the wilderness (Luke 3:1-2).

And the word of God that John the Baptist preached in the wilderness was a word of repentance, a word from God calling people to turn away from their sins and turn back to God—a word of grace to those lost in wilderness, a word of grace for those drifting too far from the shore. Moreover, John the Baptist's preaching was accompanied by "a baptism of repentance for the forgiveness of sins." Luke emphasizes that this all fulfilled a prophecy given many centuries earlier by the great Old Testament prophet Isaiah, who had foretold that John the Baptist would be "The voice of one crying out in the wilderness: 'Prepare the way of the Lord, make his paths straight. Every valley shall be filled, and every mountain and hill shall be made low, and the crooked shall be made straight, and the rough ways made smooth; and all flesh shall see the salvation of God'" (Luke 3:3-6).

John the Baptist preached the same message the Old Testament prophets, including Isaiah, preached, a message that can be distilled to a one word: "repent." To repent means as we prayed in the collect for today, we ask God to "give us grace to heed their warnings and forsake our sins" (*BCP* 159). To repent means when, as the young Bob Dylan heard on that old 78 rpm record, "You are drifting too far from the shore," you "Come to Jesus today. Let him show you the way."

So what happens if we ignore God's call to repentance? What happens if we persist in drifting too far from the shore, or wandering in circles in the wilderness? Well, the consequences can be dire not only for ourselves, but for others as well.

One of the current leading Shakespearean scholars in America is Stephen Greenblatt, a professor at Harvard who has written many books. In his most recent book, *Tyrant: Shakespeare on Politics*, he examines the lives of several of Shakespeare's most notorious tyrants, including Richard III, Lear, Macbeth, and Coriolanus. All of these tyrants persisted in drifting too far from the shore, with the resulting consequences indeed being dire for themselves and others. Listen to how Stephen Greenblatt describes Richard III:

> He is pathologically narcissistic and supremely arrogant. He has a grotesque sense of entitlement, never doubting that he can do whatever he chooses. He loves to bark orders and to watch underlings scurry to carry them out. He expects absolute loyalty, but he is incapable of gratitude. The feelings of others mean nothing to him. He has no natural grace, no sense of shared humanity, no decency.

And Stephen Greenblatt is not done; he continues:

> He is not merely indifferent to the law; he hates it and takes pleasure in breaking it. He hates it because it gets in his way and because it stands for a notion of the public good that he holds in contempt. He divides the world into winners and losers. The winners arouse his regard insofar as he can use them for his own ends; the losers arouse only his scorn (53-54).

Stephen Greenblatt minces no words in describing the tyrant Richard III. And unfortunately tyrants like Richard III are not only reserved for Shakespearean plays. Yes, there can be tyrants at work, but there are also tyrants at school, tyrants at home, tyrants at the neighborhood association meetings, and yes, even tyrants in church. But lest we begin pointing fingers at the Richard IIIs in our lives, it would be wiser to look in the mirror. How often are we narcissistic and arrogant, entitled and incapable of gratitude? How often do we divide the world into winners and losers, using the winners for our advantage and scorning the losers?

Ultimately each of the tyrants in Shakespeare's plays comes to a brutal and tragic end. Macbeth, for example, after murdering everyone who stood in his way of the throne, ultimately bemoans his tyrannous efforts as "a tale told by an idiot, full of sound and fury, signifying nothing" (V.v.26-28). Later Macbeth is confronted by Macduff, whose wife and sons were among those killed by order of Macbeth. Macduff tells Macbeth what he plans on doing after killing him:

> We'll have thee, as our rarer monsters are,
> Painted upon a pole and underwrit,
>   "Here may you see the tyrant" (V.vii.55-57).

Even Macbeth would not repent. Rather, he becomes even more entrenched and cries out, "I will not yield" (V.vii.58). Macduff then kills Macbeth.

Back to *Quigley Down Under*…late in the film Elliot Marston, who had wanted Matthew Quigley to help him eliminate the Aborigines, like Macbeth, refused to repent, refused to yield. Thinking Quigley is only skilled with rifles and not revolvers he decides he is going to teach Quigley about "quick draw" shooting in a duel. To Marston's mortal surprise, Quigley draws first and shoots him and two of his cronies. As Marston lays dying, Quigley walks over, and tells him that when it came to revolvers, "I said I never had much use for one. I never said I didn't know how to use it." Quigley spins his revolver and returns it to his belt, while Marston breathes his final breath. I guess on one level the message here is, "Don't mess with Tom Selleck."

But on a deeper level, the message is that even in the wilderness, even when drifting too far from the shore, God meets us with his grace and calls us to repent, to do the exact opposite of Elliot

Marston and Macbeth, and to heed God's call to turn from what is wrong and turn back to God—to "come to Jesus today, let him show you the way"—or, as we state in the baptism service in *The Book of Common Prayer*, "turn to Jesus Christ and accept him as your Savior" and "put your whole trust in his grace and love" (302).

Jesus was not a tyrant. Instead, Jesus became a servant, who as scripture tells us "humbled himself and became obedient to the point of death—even death on a cross" (Philippians 2:8). Jesus spent his earthly life and ministry seeking and saving the lost, seeking and saving those drifting too far from the shore. Jesus himself said, "I came not to judge the world, but to save the world" (John 12:47).

Jesus did not come to judge the world, but to save the world by taking that judgment upon himself. Jesus was crucified by tyrants, and "painted upon a pole"—the cross—with a message overwrit that, instead of saying, "Here may you see the tyrant," said, "The King of the Jews." Jesus died for tyrants. Jesus died for all those drifting too far from the shore, for all those wandering in circles in the wilderness. On the cross as Isaiah foretold, all flesh saw the salvation of God.

And even now, if you ring the doorbell, you will find that there is indeed Someone home, Someone who always offers grace for those drifting too far from the shore.

Amen.

Good News in an Age of Anxiety

> *Do not worry about anything, but in everything by prayer and supplication with thanksgiving let your requests be made known to God. And the peace of God, which surpasses all understanding, will guard your hearts and your minds in Christ Jesus (Philippians 4:6-7).*

In the Name of the Father, Son, and Holy Spirit.

Thirty years ago there was popular song that became the first acapella song ever to reach number one on the Billboard charts, a song that won a Grammy for Song of the Year, a combination of reggae and jazz by vocalist Bobby McFerrin entitled, "Don't Worry, Be Happy." McFerrin was redundantly clear in this song:

> Here's a little song I wrote
> You might want to sing it note for note
> Don't worry, be happy
> In every life we have some trouble
> But when you worry you make it double
> Don't worry, be happy
> Don't worry, be happy now
> (From his 1988 album *Simple Pleasures*)

I was a sophomore in college when this song was a hit. During finals week, my classmates and I would sing it on the way to exams in an attempt to alleviate our anxiety. "Don't worry, be happy!"

But alas, in the throes of my three-hour long Quantitative Analysis final exam that song was no help at all.

We currently live in a time of great cultural anxiety—anxiety about guns, anxiety about politics, anxiety about the stock market, anxiety about social media, anxiety about health, anxiety about the environment, anxiety about family issues, on and on it goes. During the holiday season such anxieties are often magnified.

Such anxiety can lead to nervousness, insomnia, tension, increased blood pressure, and other symptoms. When anxiety reaches a particularly high level, it can even trigger occasional, or not so occasional, panic attacks, marked by increased heartrate, shortness of breath, and trembling. And I will be vulnerable and admit that I have had occasional panic attacks. They are not fun, and even songs like "Don't Worry, Be Happy," as catchy as they are, fall short.

Maybe some of you have had anxiety dreams. Some have anxiety dreams about school—not turning in a paper on time or not being able to find the classroom for a final exam. Some have anxiety dreams about sports—standing with a football at the one yard line with a wide open end zone a couple steps away but unable to move forward as defenders sprint toward you, or you're a goalie in a soccer match and the ball is rolling in slow motion toward the goal but you cannot reach it.

As a priest I am prone to occasional anxiety dreams that are quite bizarre. Usually they involve running late for a service, unable to find my vestments, unable to find my sermon notes, unable to find the sanctuary. I keep returning to my office to get my *Book of Common Prayer* and accidentally grab a volume of *Far Side* cartoons or Shakespeare plays, and then scramble back to office yet again. When I finally arrive at the sanctuary I am too late. Everyone has gone home except for a few ushers who berate me about being late—"Where have you been?"

Then I notice that the sanctuary is flooded and there are

acolytes floating on rafts while carrying torches and the gospel book and asking me, "Where is everybody?" This is always capped off with the bishop in his full regalia looking annoyed and slowly shaking his head in disapproval. Many of you have anxiety dreams too, maybe not as bizarre as mine, but equally distressing. And unfortunately there are seasons when we awake to be reminded that the real life challenges in our lives that cause real life anxiety are not dreams at all.

Last year *The New York Times Magazine* published an article entitled "America's New Anxiety Disorder" which describes our collective cultural anxiety this way:

> There's a bleakness in the atmosphere, and a consensus on what to call it: "anxiety." For the past decade or so American anxiety was usually described as either a mental health issue or a generational style. Psychologically, we were steadily becoming more apprehensive than ever, with—according to the National Institute of Mental Heath—18 percent of people experiencing actual anxiety disorders in any given year. Generationally, the whole social attitude of younger adults changed… Panicked strivers have replaced sullen slackers as the caricatures of the moment, and Xanax has eclipsed Prozac as the emblem of the national mood (Nitsuh Abebe, April 18, 2017).

While this current cultural anxiety is pronounced, it is not a new phenomenon. Seventy years ago W. H. Auden entitled in his 1948 Pulitzer Prize winning poem "The Age of Anxiety." Each age in its own way is an age of anxiety.

Paul's Letter to the Philippians contains good news for our age of anxiety:

> Do not worry about anything, but in everything by prayer and supplication with thanksgiving let your requests be made known to God. And the peace of God, which surpasses all understanding, will

guard your hearts and your minds in Christ Jesus (Philippians 4:6-7).

When Paul wrote these words he was imprisoned in Rome, suffering for the gospel. In his Second Letter to the Corinthians, Paul vulnerably revealed that even he was not immune to anxiety: "And, besides other things, I am under pressure because of my anxiety for all the churches. Who is weak, and I am not weak?" (2 Corinthians 11:28-29). And yet even though Paul was honest about his struggles with anxiety he still knew the best way to address it: pray—ask God for help—"by prayer and supplication with thanksgiving let your requests be made known to God." And what happens when we do that? God gives us peace—"the peace of God which surpasses understanding"—to guard our hearts and minds.

Broadly speaking, all of Paul's thirteen New Testament letters are roughly divided into two parts: what God has done for us and what we are called to do in response. Earlier in his Letter to the Philippians Paul wrote that the same God who began a work in our lives will finish it (1:6), that Jesus died for us on the cross and was raised again (2:8-9), that Jesus will come again to complete his work of salvation (3:20-21). In response to all God has already done, is doing, and will do, we are called to deal with our anxiety by prayer, by asking this same God for help.

When I was a junior in high school, a girl whom I had been dating for a long time in high school terms, six whole weeks, broke up with me via a note written to me by a friend of hers—perhaps the equivalent of being "dumped" in a text today. Moreover, this was three days before taking the dreaded SAT exam, which as a teacher told me, was no reason to stress because the SAT only impacted where I may go to college and therefore perhaps where I may meet my future spouse and therefore whether and what kind of kids I may have and what career I may pursue and where I may end up living the rest of my life…but no reason to stress.

That evening a youth minister at our church pointed out today's passage to me, and encouraged me to take my anxiety to the Lord in prayer. I did, and it helped, but on the way to take the SAT I made the mistake of stopping by 7-Eleven for a Big Gulp Mountain Dew so when the test administrator later refused to let me go to the restroom I began wrestling with a different kind of anxiety…oh well.

In the middle of the nineteenth century, another age of anxiety in an America on the cusp of the Civil War, a hymn was written by Joseph Scriven that has gone on to become a beloved hymn, and one I wish were included in our hymnal, a hymn that beautifully describes what Paul writes in today's passage:

> What a friend we have in Jesus, all our sins and griefs to bear
> What a privilege to carry everything to God in prayer
> O what peace we often forfeit, O what needless pain we bear
> All because we do not carry everything to God in prayer
> Have we trials and temptations, is there trouble anywhere
> We should never be discouraged, take it to the Lord in prayer
> Can we find a friend so faithful who will all our sorrows share
> Jesus knows our every weakness, take it to the Lord in prayer

The cynical may dismiss this powerful hymn as a simple-minded prescription or an emotional Band-Aid, but it actually is a reminder of the best thing to do with anxiety—take it to the Lord in prayer—as scripture also tells us, to "cast all your anxiety on [God] because he cares for you" (1 Peter 5:7).

The greatest theologian of the twentieth century was the Swiss theologian Karl Barth, whose magnum opus entitled *Church Dogmatics*, is over six million words long and took him over thirty years to write. He wrote during the years of the Third Reich, World War II, and the Cold War, all ages of intense collective anxiety. In a smaller book called *Dogmatics in Outline* Barth wrote:

> The greatest hindrance to faith again and again is the anxiety and pride of our human hearts. We would rather not live by grace. Something within us energetically rebels against it. We do not wish to receive grace…this swing to and fro between pride and anxiety is man's life. Faith bursts through them both… We may hold *entirely* to God's Word (20-21).

The reason "we may hold entirely to God's Word" is because God is already holding us.

In my office there are several pieces of furniture—two desks, five chairs, several bookshelves, an antique table—but the most important piece of furniture in my office is a prayer desk. While some days I forget, most days I spend some time kneeling at that prayer desk, taking the things that cause anxiety in my life to the Lord in prayer. And the most common prayer I pray is actually only one word long, "Help"—asking God to help, to do what I can't do, to solve what I can't solve, to give me wisdom and clarity where I need it—whether it's for my own life and family, or for the myriad and sundry aspects of church life.

And often, what Paul describes as "the peace of God which surpasses all understanding" indeed begins to guard my heart and mind anew. Somehow God reassures me that ultimately he will take care of it, whatever that "it" may be. And I drink another cup of coffee from a mug that a friend at Christ Church gave me that says, "I got this - God."

The "peace of God which passes all understanding" is that even though on the surface there is no change at all in any of the things causing you anxiety, you have this sense that God has indeed got it, that it is going to be okay.

In the Garden of Gethsemane, Jesus faced anxiety we could never imagine: "Father, if you are willing, remove this cup from me; yet not my will, but yours be done." As the horrors of Good Friday loomed ever nearer, scripture tells us, "In his anguish he prayed more earnestly, and his sweat became like great drops of blood falling down on the ground" (Luke 22:42, 44). And yet as he drew his final breath on the cross, Jesus cast all his cares on his Heavenly Father, "Father into your hands I commend my spirit" (Luke 23:46). And the Risen Jesus, the Prince of Peace, offers you peace today, "peace which passes all understanding" to guard your heart and mind—real grace for the real anxiety in your real life.

The gospel is good news in an age of anxiety, good news for those who need more than "Don't worry, be happy." Jesus knows your every weakness, take it to the Lord in prayer, because God's word to you today is…"I got this."

Amen.

God Lifts Up the Lowly

He has brought down the powerful from their thrones, and lifted up the lowly (Luke 1:52).

In the Name of the Father, Son, and Holy Spirit.

You are ten years old and in fifth grade. It is a crisp fall Saturday afternoon in Northern Virginia. You arrive at a soccer field for a game against your biggest rival, a team with a bunch of kids you know from school, including a few notorious bullies. You have recently started going to church so the fact that you literally hate the other team makes you feel a little guilty, but not that guilty. There is a kid on your team named Tommy. Tommy wears very thick glasses, and his dirty blonde hair is an unkempt mess, cowlicks in all directions. Tommy has a form of cerebral palsy that has affected his left arm, which is smaller than his right arm and always bent at the elbow, his hand hanging limp. His arm and hand swing back and forth as he runs. Tommy has never scored a goal, and thinks he never will.

For years Tommy has had this disability. For years Tommy has been teased because of it, even though of course he can't help it, and today is no exception. As your team warms up on your side of the field, you and Tommy are passing a ball back and forth when the goalie on the other team begins taunting Tommy, holding his left arm and hand just like Tommy's and shouting insults at him. Tommy's face turns red, and you say to him, "Shake it off, Tommy." Tommy won't make eye contact (he never makes eye contact) and replies, "I'm tired of shaking it off."

The game is heated, lots of dirty plays, lots of "talking smack." Late in the game it is tied 2 - 2, and the other team has a goal kick. Their obnoxious goalie, who has been taunting Tommy the whole game, sets the ball down for the goal kick, and while walking backwards holds his left arm up in continued mockery of Tommy, then runs forward and kicks the ball…and yes, the ball happens to go right toward Tommy. Without even thinking about it, Tommy, his left arm swinging limp, swings his right leg at the ball, and completes a perfect half volley (when you kick the ball the split second it bounces off the ground, like a dropkick in football). You watch the goalie stare in horror at the ball Tommy has just kicked as it sails over his head and right under the crossbar for a spectacular goal.

Your team erupts. Your sideline erupts. Tommy is jumping up and down in joy his left arm flinging around. When the game ends a few minutes later, you have defeated your arch rivals 3 – 2 thanks to Tommy's amazing goal. Your team surrounds Tommy and he is beaming with joy, and he is no longer avoiding eye contact. The next week at school everyone passing Tommy in the halls, except the members of the other team of course, give kudos to Tommy, who is holding up his head for the first time that you can remember. One day at lunch that week he tells you that goal was one of the best moments of his life. And as you look back on it forty years later you realize it was one of the best moments of your life too.

On this Fourth Sunday of Advent the gospel passage includes one of the high water marks of scripture, a psalm of praise spoken by someone else who, like Tommy, was lowly, Mary. Mary was pregnant with the Son of God, but of course had been insulted and mocked for being pregnant out of wedlock. Mary was from a poor family in a poor town called Nazareth. And yet God had given grace to Mary, and Mary knew it. In a psalm of praise known as the Magnificat she begins, "My soul magnifies the Lord, and my spirit rejoices in God my Savior, for he has looked with favor on the lowliness of his servant" (Luke 1:46-48). God had looked with favor, or you could say God had given grace, to the lowliness of Mary—and in response she praised God. Later in the Magnificat, Mary proclaims that God "has brought down the powerful from their thrones, and lifted up the lowly" (Luke 1:52).

The gospel is good news for the lowly, because as Mary proclaimed, God indeed has "lifted up the lowly"—and God still does.

The Greek word translated "lowly" in this passage could also be translated as "humble" or "downcast" (like someone who never makes eye contact). God does not give a self-help book to the lowly, or tell the lowly to shake it off. Instead, God gives grace to the lowly. Instead, God lifts up the lowly.

What Mary describes in the Magnificat as God bringing down the powerful from their thrones and lifting up the lowly is a recurring theme in scripture. In the Old Testament, God brought down the pharaoh of Egypt and lifted up lowly Israel out of four centuries of slavery. Later God brought down King Saul and lifted up a lowly and rejected shepherd named David to the throne of Israel.

Along these lines, twice in the New Testament we read that God opposes the proud and gives grace to the lowly, or humble. In his epistle James writes "God opposes the proud, but gives grace to the humble" (James 4:6) and in his first epistle Peter echoes this and takes is a step further, "God opposes the proud, but gives grace to the humble. Humble yourselves therefore under the mighty hand of God, so that he may exalt you (or lift you up) in due time" (1 Peter 5:5). The Greek word for "humble" in both those verses is the same word translated "lowly" in today's gospel passage. God gives grace to the humble. God lifts up the lowly.

On May 7, 2015 one of my favorite actors, Denzel Washington, gave a moving commencement speech at Dillard University in New Orleans. He spoke about his personally experiencing how God lifts up the lowly:

> Everything that you think you see in me, everything that I've accomplished, everything that you think I have, and I have a few things, everything that I have is by the grace of God. Understand that. It's a gift. March 27, 1975 was forty years ago. I was flunking out of college. I had a 1.7 grade point average. I hope none of you can relate. I was sitting in my mother's beauty parlor and I'm looking in the mirror and I see behind me this woman under a dryer and she was looking at me. And she said, "Somebody give me a pen, I have a prophecy." March 27, 1975. She said, "Boy, you are gonna travel the world and speak to millions of people." Now mind you, I had flunked out of college, I'm thinking about joining the army, I didn't know what I was going to do. She's telling me I'm gonna travel the world and speak to millions of people. Well, I have traveled the world, and I have spoken to millions of people…and God has kept me humble. I didn't always stick with him but he always stuck with me.

He later adds, "Finally, I pray that you put your slippers way under the bed tonight, so that when you wake up in the morning, you have to get on your knees to reach them, and while you're down there, say 'Thank you for grace.'"

When Mary proclaimed that God "has brought down the powerful from their thrones, and lifted up the lowly," she was not just speaking about herself, but for all the lowly in the world. The truth is we are all lowly in one way or another. And yet even when we don't always stick with God, God always sticks with us.

Even if externally we may appear successful, internally we may be experiencing something quite different. For example, in her 2014 book *Yes Please* comedienne and television producer Amy Poehler vulnerably writes about how hard we can be on ourselves, especially when it comes to our appearance:

> I hate how I look. That is the mantra we repeat over and over again. Sometimes we whisper it quietly and other times we shout it out loud in front of a mirror. I hate how I look. I hate how my face looks my body looks I am too fat or too skinny or too tall or too wide or my legs are stupid and my face is too smiley or my teeth are dumb and my nose is serious and my stomach is being so lame... You are six or twelve or fifteen and you look in the mirror and you hear a voice so awful and mean it takes your breath away. It tells you that you are fat and ugly and you don't deserve love. And the scary part is the demon is your own voice. But it doesn't sound like you. It sounds like a strangled and seductive version of you. Think Darth Vader or an angry Lauren Bacall... The bad news is it never goes away (15-16).

But even if that demon voice never goes away, there is Someone Else who also never goes away, the God of grace who lifts up the lowly, who assures you that even if you don't think you deserve love, you still are loved—that regardless of what you think of your appearance, regardless of whether or not you have an arm hanging limp by your side, you are loved by God, you are lifted up by God.

"God has brought down the powerful from their thrones, and lifted up the lowly." That statement of Mary is also a powerful summary of the gospel. Except with the gospel, Jesus, who is omnipotent, all-powerful, was not brought down from his throne in heaven by someone else, but rather willingly stepped down from it of his own volition. In Jesus Christ, the God of all grace, humbled himself and became incarnate on your behalf. Scripture tells us that Jesus Christ, "emptied himself, taking the form of a slave, being born in human likeness" and "humbled himself and became obedient to the point of death—even death on a cross" (Philippians 2:7-8). Jesus literally said, "Come to me, all you that are weary and are carrying heavy hardens, and I will give you rest. Take my yoke upon you and learn from me; for I am gentle and *humble* (or "lowly"—same word Mary used) in heart, and you will find rest for your souls" (Matthew 11:28-29, italics added). The God who gives grace to the humble literally humbled himself for you.

Moreover, the God who gives grace to the humble is the same God who lifts up the lowly, and the same God who was literally lifted up on the cross for you. Jesus himself proclaimed, "And I, when I am lifted up from the earth, will draw all people to myself" (John 12:32).

Jesus allowed himself to be lifted up on the cross in order to lift up all the lowly of the world.

That is what happened on Good Friday, when Jesus was lifted on the cross to atone for the sins of the world, taking the lowliest position in order to lift up all the lowly in the world, to make eye contact with all the lowly in the world and say, "You are loved, you are forgiven, you are lifted up. You will travel the world. You will speak to millions of people. You will score spectacular goals over those who have made fun of you for things you cannot help."

And on Easter morning God the Father through the power of the Holy Spirit lifted Jesus up out of the grave and "exalted him and gave him the name that is above every name, so that at the name of Jesus every knee should bend, in heaven and on earth and under the earth, and every tongue should confess that Jesus Christ is Lord" (Philippians 2:9).

Scripture tells us Jesus humbled himself and "was handed over to death for our trespasses and was raised for our justification" (Romans 4:25). In other words, Jesus died on the cross for you and Jesus was raised from the dead for you.

Jesus became lowly in order to lift up all the lowly of the world.

And even now God lifts up the lowly—that is the good news of the gospel.

In response we can kneel and pray, "Thank you for grace."

Amen.

The Rising of the Grace of God

A Christmas Sermon

> *In that region there were shepherds living in the fields, keeping watch over their flock by night. Then an angel of the Lord stood before them, and the glory of the Lord shone round about them, and they were terrified. But the angel said to them, "Do not be afraid; for see—I am bringing you good news of great joy for all the people; to you is born this day in the city of David a Savior, who is the Messiah, the Lord. This will be a sign for you; you will find a child wrapped in bands of cloth and lying in a manger." And suddenly there was with the angel a multitude of the heavenly host, praising God and saying, "Glory to God in the highest heaven, and on earth peace among those whom he favors!" When the angels had left them and gone into heaven, the shepherds said to one another, "Let us go now to Bethlehem and see this thing that has taken place, which the Lord has made known to us." So they went with haste and found Mary and Joseph, and the child lying in the manger (Luke 2:8-16).*

In the Name of the Father, Son, and Holy Spirit.

So glad to worship with you this Christmas! I'm going to begin by juxtaposing an episode of the classic television comedy *The Office* and a song Bruce Springsteen performed as part of his acclaimed solo concert series on Broadway this year.

In the Christmas episode of the second season of *The Office* Michael Scott, the manager of the Scranton, Pennsylvania, branch of the Dunder Mifflin Paper Company, is wearing a Santa hat and enthusiastically proclaims, "Presents are the best way to show someone how much you care. It is like this tangible thing that you can point to and say, 'Hey man, I love you this many dollars' worth.'"

Later in the episode the office staff is exchanging their Secret Santa gifts. Michael had gone way overboard on his gift for Ryan, who opens his present, "Whoa, a video iPod." Michael confesses, "Someone really got carried away with the spirit of Christmas… It was me, I got carried away with the spirit." Ryan feels really uncomfortable, "Wasn't there a $20 limit on the gift? This is four hundred bucks." "You don't know that," Michael replies. "Uh, yeah, you left the price tag on." Michael acts surprised: "I did? Oh well, who cares? It doesn't matter what I spent. What matters is that Christmas is fun, right?"

The awkward tension is palpable as the neurotic Dwight Schrute, wearing elf ears and elf hat, hands Michael his present. Michael grins, "Oh hey, for me!" and unwraps it, "What's in here?" It's an oven mitt. Michael puts it on and is so disappointed: "Ah, come on." Phyllis pipes up, "I knitted it for you!" He holds it up and glares at Phyllis, "An oven mitt?" Michael then storms out, tossing his Santa hat onto a couch and complains, "So Phyllis is basically saying, 'Hey Michael, I know you did a lot to help the office this year but I only care about you a homemade oven mitt's worth.' I gave Ryan an iPod!" Michael then returns and changes Secret Santa into Yankee Swap, which only makes things worse and turns the whole office gift exchange into a train wreck. Of course in South Georgia, Yankee Swap would never work simply because it's called Yankee Swap.

A couple weeks ago Bruce Springsteen completed the last of 236 performances of his highly acclaimed solo acoustic concert series "Springsteen on Broadway," summarizing his legendary five-decade career in music, which he has described as his "long and noisy prayer." Near the end of each performance he sang a haunting version of "The Rising," a song he wrote in the wake of 9/11, a song effusive with hope. He begins:

> Can't see nothin' in front of me
> Can't see nothin' coming up behind
> Make my way through this darkness
> I can't feel nothin' but this chain that binds me
> Lost track of how far I've gone
> How far I've gone, how far I've climbed
> On my back's a sixty pound stone
> On my shoulder a half mile of line
> Come on up for the rising
> Come on up, lay your hands in mine
> Come on up for the rising
> Come on up for the rising tonight

Springsteen then sings about what many of us do when can't see in front of us or behind us, what we do as we make our way through the darkness with whatever chains bind us—he sings about looking up at the sky:

> Sky of blackness and sorrow
> Sky of love, sky of tears
> Sky of glory and sadness
> Sky of mercy, sky of fear
> Sky of memory and shadow
> Your burnin' wind fills my arms tonight
> Sky of longing and emptiness
> Sky of fullness, sky of blessed life...
> Come on up for the rising
> Come on up for the rising tonight
> (Title track of his 2002 album *The Rising*)

The world is full of people who feel lost in the darkness, who cannot see what is behind them or in front of them, who feel weighed down by chains that bind them, chains perhaps only God knows about. Numerous studies have demonstrated that the current generation of Millennials is the most anxious generation in American history. As we near the close of what has been a particularly stressful year for many people, as trite as it may sound, we need more than an oven mitt, even more than a $400 video iPod or a game of Yankee Swap. We need the gospel.

Christmas is all about the gospel, the good news that God loves us so much he sent his Son Jesus Christ to save us. Every year on Christmas we read about what the shepherds saw when they looked up at the sky on "the night of our dear savior's birth":

> In that region there were shepherds living in the fields, keeping watch over their flock by night. Then an angel of the Lord stood before then, and the glory of the Lord shone round about them, and they were terrified. But the angel said to them, "Do not be afraid; for see—I am bringing you good news of great joy for all the people; to you is born this day in the city of David a Savior, who is the Messiah, the Lord. This will be a sign for you; you will find a child wrapped in bands of cloth and lying in a manger" (Luke 2:8-12).

The shepherds looked up into a "sky of fullness, a sky of blessed life" as the angels proclaimed the rising of the grace of God—the rising of the grace of God for those who cannot see anything behind them or in front of them, the rising of the grace of God for those who only feel the chains that bind them, the rising of the grace of God for anxious Millennials, the rising of the grace of God for the whole world.

The shepherds saw the sky filled with angels proclaiming, "Glory to God in the highest heaven, and on earth peace among those whom he favors!" You could also translate "on earth peace among those whom he favors" as "on earth peace among those whom he gives grace"—the favor of God is the grace of the God, the rising of the grace of God—and those whom God favors includes you.

Then the shepherds hurried to Bethlehem and "found Mary and Joseph, and the child lying in the manger" (Luke 2:13-16). There the shepherds saw Love personified, our newborn savior Jesus Christ, there the shepherds saw what we sing in "Silent Night": "the dawn of redeeming grace."

This past week *BBC News* published an article about Christmas grace:

> A family was left shocked to find their late elderly neighbor had left Christmas presents to give to their (two year old) daughter (Cadi) for the next fourteen years. Ken, who was in his late 80's, lived near Owen and Caroline Williams for the last two years. The couple said Ken "doted" on their two-year-old daughter Cadi. He died recently and on Monday evening, his daughter knocked on the Williams' home to deliver the presents.
>
> "She was clutching this big plastic sack and I thought it was rubbish she was going to ask me to throw out," said Mr. Williams. "But she said it was everything her dad had put away for Cadi, all of the Christmas presents he had bought for her. I brought it back in and my wife was on FaceTime to her mum in Ireland. My wife started to tear up and I started to tear up, and her mum started to tear up. It's difficult describing it because it was so unexpected" (December 22, 2018).

Who knows? Maybe one of Cadi's presents will be an oven mitt. What Owen Williams said though about their late neighbor's grace for Cadi is true about the gospel of the rising grace of God for all of us: it's difficult describing it because it is so unexpected.

As absurd as Michael Scott of *The Office* could be, there is an element of truth when he said presents are "like this tangible thing that you can point to and say, 'Hey man, I love you this many dollars' worth'" because the gospel is about "a tangible thing you can point to," or rather, a tangible Person you can point to by whom God says, "I love you this much." On Christmas night the rising grace of God was manifested in the unexpected form of a newborn baby. Jesus himself said, "God so loved the world that he gave his only Son, so that everyone who believes in him may not perish but may have eternal life" (John 3:16).

And on Good Friday, the rising grace of God was manifested again in an unexpected way as this same newborn baby, now a grown man, gave his life on the cross for you, swapped places with you, to ensure that year after year not just for the next fourteen years but for the next fourteen millions years and beyond, you will receive the grace of God.

On Good Friday above the cross the same sky in which the angels had earlier sung, "Glory to God in the highest heaven, and earth peace among those whom he favors" had become "a sky of blackness and sorrow, a sky of love, sky of tears, sky of glory and sadness, sky of mercy, sky of fear"—but above all "a sky of blessed life." And after his death Jesus, who as a baby had been "wrapped in bands of cloth" and placed in a manger was once again "wrapped in bands of cloth" but this time placed in a tomb. And then the rising grace of God appeared in in yet another unexpected way, by the rising of Jesus from the dead on Easter morning.

Some may dismiss the gospel as a "big plastic sack" of rubbish to throw out, but be careful what you throw out, because the gospel is actually the good news of the unexpected grace of God.

So this Christmas, even as you continue to make your way through the darkness in your life, remember that the Risen Jesus is in front of you and behind you, the Risen Jesus is there to break the chains that bind you—and the Risen Jesus is beckoning you to come on up for the rising grace of God.

Amen.

Grace and Truth Came through Jesus Christ

The law indeed was given through Moses; grace and truth came through Jesus Christ (John 1:17).

In the Name of the Father, Son, and Holy Spirit.

Every year the appointed gospel passage for the First Sunday after Christmas is the prologue from the Gospel According to John, one of the most beautifully written and theologically loaded passages in the entire Bible. John begins by famously describing the divinity of Jesus Christ, the Son of God, to whom he refers as "the Word":

> In the beginning was the Word, and the Word was with God, and the Word was God. He was in the beginning with God. All things came into being through him, and without him not one thing came into being. What has come into being in him was life, and the life was the light of all people (John 1:1-4).

Throughout his account of the gospel John returns repeatedly to the idea of Jesus being both life and light, both "the way, the truth and the life" (14:6) and "the light of the world" (8:12). John also tells us that Jesus, the Word, fully divine, became fully human at his incarnation: "The Word became flesh and lived among us, and we have seen his glory, the glory as of a father's only son, full of grace and truth...From his fullness we have all received grace upon grace" (1:14, 16).

And then John summarizes the entire Bible in one verse: "The law indeed was given through Moses; grace and truth came through Jesus Christ" (John 1:17). The Old Testament is centered on the law—the moral law distilled in the Ten Commandments and the sacrificial law concerning the atonement for sin. God's law was given to help us honor God and other people, to protect us from the destructive consequences of sin. Over and over again the narrative of the Old Testament is the recurring cycle of God's people breaking God's law, getting into serious trouble as a result, repenting, being rescued by God, and then breaking God's law again and beginning the cycle anew. All the words of the Old Testament prophets can be summed up in one word: repent, stop breaking God's law and turn back to God. "The law indeed was given through Moses."

"Grace and truth came through Jesus Christ"—that is the message of the New Testament. The Old Testament is centered on the law of God. The New Testament is centered on the grace of God, grace given all of us in Jesus Christ. "Grace and truth came through Jesus Christ"—that is why we emphasize God's grace here at Christ Church more than anything else. The center of the gospel is the grace of God.

God's grace is unconditional love. One definition of grace is "unmerited favor," which is true, but grace is much more than that, as Paul Zahl describes in his book *Grace in Practice*:

> What is grace? Grace is love that seeks you out when you have nothing to give in return. Grace is love coming at you that has nothing to do with you. Grace is being loved when you are unlovable. It is being loved when you are the opposite of lovable...It reflects a decision on the part of the giver, the one who loves, in relation to the receiver, the one who is loved, that

negates any qualifications the receiver may personally hold… Grace is irrational in the sense that it has nothing to do with weights and measures... Grace is *one-way love* (36).

Whether or not she was aware of it, Taylor Swift was singing about grace when she sang, "You told me I was pretty when I looked like a mess" (from "Today was a Fairytale"). Bono, the lead singer of U2 was fully aware of it when he sang, "Grace—she takes the blame, she covers the shame, removes the stain…grace makes beauty out of ugly things" (from "Grace").

Last week *The New York Times* published an op-ed by entitled "The Uncommon Power of Grace" in which the writer observes:

> We are naturally drawn to covenants and karma, to cause and effect, to earning what we receive. Grace is different. It is the unmerited favor of God, unconditional love given to the undeserving. It's a difficult concept to understand because it isn't entirely rational…there's a radical equality at the core of grace. None of us are deserving of God's grace, so it's not dependent on social status, wealth, or intelligence. There is equality between kings and peasants, the prominent and the unheralded, rule followers and rule breakers.

And this grace of God makes a real difference in people's real lives:

> You don't sense hard edges, dogmatism, or self-righteous judgment from gracious people. There's a tenderness about them that opens doors that had previously been bolted shut. People who have been transformed by grace have a special place in their hearts for those living in the shadows of society. They're easily moved by stories of suffering and step into the breach to heal. And grace properly understood always produces gratitude (Peter Wehner, December 23, 2018).

Grace is one of the central themes in the beautiful and highly acclaimed 2018 foreign film *Roma*. The main character is Cleo Gutierrez, a maid for the wealthy de Tavira family in early 1970s Mexico City. The film begins with a lengthy shot of water being poured onto the floor of a porch that Cleo is cleaning, with Cleo in control of where the water goes. Cleo is not only the maid, she is also the unheralded caretaker of several young children—she cooks for them, cleans their clothes, takes them to and from school, bathes them, and helps them to bed at night. Every day, all day, Cleo is a servant who does more than her job; she gives grace to the de Tavira family.

Near the end of the film the de Tavira family, absent the father, is at the beach. Cleo warns the children again and again about not going too far into the ocean, but the children defy Cleo's warnings, as children are apt to do, and go way too far out. When she realizes they are in danger, even though she does not know how to swim and is frightened of the ocean, Cleo makes her way through the heavy surf and the rough waves. She is absolutely terrified of the water, but even more terrified of losing the children. She has no control of where the water goes.

Cleo keeps going, risking her life with every step into deeper surf, until she reaches the children. She manages to rescue the children who were unable to rescue themselves. The entire sequence is filmed in one spectacular camera shot, brilliant cinematography. After Cleo has brought the children back to safety, they all huddle together on the shore and hold onto each other—all grateful to be safely on shore, all grateful to Cleo, the unheralded servant, for saving the children's lives.

The law did not work in this instance because the children defied the law. But grace worked, the grace of Cleo saved the children.

I literally experienced something very similar when I was eight years old. My family was at Virginia Beach for a week, the first time I could remember seeing the ocean. My dad rented a raft for me and I spent all day riding wave after wave after wave back to shore. The next day I began again, but kept going a little farther out, even though I had been warned about it. And you can guess what happened—a rip current suddenly swept me out really far from shore.

I remember paddling as hard as I could but I was not getting any closer to the shore. A lifeguard stood atop his large white wooden lifeguard chair and blew his whistle repeatedly, waving his arms at me to come back to shore. But I couldn't. I even slid off the raft and tried doggy paddling while pulling the raft by the white cord, but to no avail, and when I thought about the movie *Jaws* I immediately scurried back atop the raft. I was unable to help myself, and I was really scared.

Finally a different lifeguard swam out me. As he drew near I slid off the raft because I thought he and I could tag team, work together to save me, because I wanted to "do my part." When he arrived he smiled and said, "I've got you buddy, it's gonna be okay, just get back on the raft." I did, and he brought me back to shore. I was unable to rescue myself. That lifeguard rescued me. The law did not work because I defied the warnings about going too far out, and when I was waved back in I could not do it. I needed to be saved, and thankfully I was.

"The law indeed was given through Moses; grace and truth came through Jesus Christ." When it comes to your salvation, to your relationship with God, the law does not work, but the grace of God does.

So how did Jesus relate to the law?

First, when it came to the Old Testament law, Jesus did not water it down; instead, he turned up the heat, as he preached in his Sermon on the Mount:

> You have heard that it was said to those of ancient

times, "You shall not murder"; and "whoever murders shall be liable to judgment." But I say to you that if you are angry with a brother or sister, you will be liable to judgement; and if you insult a brother or sister, you will be liable to the council; and if you say, "You fool," you will be liable to the hell of fire (Matthew 5:21-22).

Second, Jesus summarized the entire Old Testament law in one word: love:

"You shall love the Lord your God with all your heart, and with all your soul, and with all your mind." This is the greatest and first commandment. And a second is like it: "You shall love your neighbor as yourself." On these two commandments hang all the law and the prophets (Matthew 22:37-40).

And finally, Jesus fulfilled the law in our place, as he said he would:

Do not think that I have come to abolish the law or the prophets; I have come not to abolish but to fulfill. For truly I tell you, until heaven and earth pass away, not one letter, not one stroke of a letter, will pass from the law until all is accomplished (Matthew 5:17-18).

And on Good Friday the grace of God that came in Jesus Christ was manifested in a way no one saw coming as Jesus, the Word of God—fully divine, fully human—died on the cross to fulfill the law. Jesus, by his love, on which hung "all the law and the prophets," died to save you as he himself hung on the cross. When it comes to the sin in your life Jesus has taken the blame, covered the shame and removed the stain. Even though he was terrified Jesus waded into the dangerous surf of sin and death all the way until he reached us and in his death and resurrection he brought us back to shore. Scripture tells us plainly, "God proves his love for us in that while we were still sinners Christ died for us" (Romans 5:8).

"The law indeed was given through Moses; grace and truth

came through Jesus Christ"—scripture tells us and that "Christ is the end of the law" (Romans 10:4) and that "you are not under law but under grace" (Romans 6:14). And every time we have a baptism we are reminded that through the death and resurrection of Jesus Christ you have been forgiven your sins and raised to "the new life of grace" (*BCP* 308).

The law did not work, but grace did…and still does.

As you begin a new calendar year this week, may you experience wave after wave after wave of God's grace.

Amen.

Jesus Saves the Best for Last

On the third day there was a wedding in Cana of Galilee, and the mother of Jesus was there. Jesus and his disciples had also been invited to the wedding. When the wine gave out, the mother of Jesus said to him, "They have no wine." And Jesus said to her, "Woman, what concern is that to you and to me? My hour has not yet come." His mother said to his servants, "Do whatever he tells you." Now standing there were six stone water jars for the Jewish rites of purification, each holding twenty or thirty gallons. Jesus said to them, "Fill the jars with water." And they filled them up to the brim. He said to them, "Now draw some out, and take it to the chief steward." So they took it. When the steward tasted the water that had become wine, and did not know where it came from (though the servants who had drawn the water knew), the steward called the bridegroom and said to him, "Everyone serves the good wine first, and then the inferior wine after the guests have become drunk. But you have kept the good wine until now." Jesus did this, the first of his signs, in Cana of Galilee, and revealed his glory; and his disciples believed in him (John 2:1-11).

In the Name of the Father, Son, and Holy Spirit.

The Apostle John structured his account of the gospel around seven signs, or miracles, Jesus performed, each of which revealed in a different way his glory as the Son of God. Today's gospel lesson recounts the first of these seven signs: Jesus' changing water into wine at a wedding in Cana of Galilee.

For many of us, our wedding day is one of the most important and memorable days of our lives. And yet in spite of all the planning, weddings often contain some unexpected moments. After Steph and I married on a scorching July afternoon, as we rode in a limo to the reception she had a glass of champagne and I, so excited and happy that I was not paying attention, polished off the rest of the bottle. Steph asked for some more, but…there was no more—oops. Shortly thereafter at the receiving line each person appeared to me as three people, all blurred and wobbly, and I tried my best to smile at the "middle" person and shake the "middle" hand proffered to me as they said, "Congratulations! Lovely wedding, just lovely!"

Once I presided at a wedding where the bride and bridesmaids got stuck in traffic, and I spent a very tense 45 minutes with the groom and groomsmen waiting in the narthex in a remote country church with no cell phone coverage. Thankfully they all eventually arrived. At another wedding I presided, when we got to the part of the liturgy when the priest says, "If any of you can show just cause why they may not be married lawfully, speak now; or else for ever hold your peace," someone actually spoke up. A (how do I put this politely?) extremely inebriated gentleman stood up in the back of the congregation holding up a beer and did his best Larry the Cable Guy impression and shouted, "Let's get-r-done!" Classy.

Some weddings have an expected moment that does not happen, like the very first wedding I performed when I forgot to say, "You may kiss the bride"…a wedding with no kiss…because there is not a rubric for it in the prayer book, and I had gone "by the book." Needless to say, I added that rubric to my prayer book.

As some of you may have seen online, last month there was a

wedding in Alabama at which something unexpected happened. The bride, Mary Bourne Roberts, gently guided her wheelchair bound father, Jim Roberts, who was in the final stages of incurable brain cancer, out onto the dancefloor for the bride/father dance. Jim was wearing a grey tuxedo with a white rose boutonniere. Mary Bourne, a professional dance instructor, held his hands and beautifully danced to the title track of Lee Ann Womack's 2000 country album *I Hope You Dance*. As Mary Bourne held her father's hands she swayed and sashayed and twirled, an incessant smile beaming from her face the whole time, as you heard these lyrics being sung:

> I hope you never fear those mountains in the distance
> Never settle for the path of least resistance
> Living might mean taking chances but they're worth taking
> Loving might be a mistake but it's worth making
> Don't let some hell-bent heart leave you bitter
> When you come close to selling out, reconsider
> Give the heavens more than just a passing glance
> And when you get the choice to sit it out or dance
> I hope you dance

At the end of the dance, Mary Bourne gave her father a big hug and kiss, as he beamed back at her, his eyes brimming with tears. Mary Bourne later said, "We had always planned to use the song. We weren't sure how he was even going to feel that day. We just knew that we were going to do it somehow." And they did.

At the wedding in today's gospel passage something unexpected happened: "the wine gave out." Running out of wine at a wedding in biblical times was a major faux pas. Mary tells her son Jesus, "They have no wine," and Jesus responds in a curious way: "Woman, what concern is that to you and to me? My hour has not yet come." First of all, lest you think Jesus was being rude and dismissive to his own mother, the Aramaic word for "woman" he used was a term of respect and honor, albeit not one we would use with our mothers today. Later Jesus would address his mother in the same way, and later, what Jesus meant by "My hour has not yet come" would be made clear. But Mary knew Jesus would do something to help with the wine running out, which is why she told him in the first place…and also why she told the servants, "Do whatever he tells you" (John 2:1-5).

(As a side note, Mary's words to the servants, "Do whatever he tells you," is sound advice for all of us when you sense the Lord telling you to do something, like apologize to that person you know you offended, or help out that person you know is in need, or let go of that grudge you have been nursing for years).

Then Jesus himself does something unexpected. He tells the servants to fill up the "six stone water jars" with water, each of which, as John noted, held "twenty or thirty gallons." The servants did so. In fact, "they filled them up to the brim" (John 2:6-7). (Another side note, metaphorically if the Lord tells you to fill up some water jars, don't "sort of" fill them; fill them "up to the brim").

Then Jesus told the servants, "No draw some out, and take it to the chief steward." They did just that, and the water had been changed wine, not watered down cheap wine but top-shelf wine, wine so good the steward said, "Everyone serves the good wine first, and then the inferior wine after the guests have become drunk. But you have kept the good wine until now" (John 2:8-10). In other words, Jesus saved the best for last. There were 120 to 180 gallons of top-shelf wine. It must have been an Episcopal wedding. It certainly was not a Southern Baptist wedding.

John then concludes this passage: "Jesus did this, the first of his signs, in Cana of Galilee, and revealed his glory; and his disciples believed in him" (John 2:11). John goes on to record six more signs Jesus did, each of which also "revealed his glory" as the Son of God.

Jesus healed a little boy who was dying (John 4:46-54), healed a lame man who had been unable to walk for thirty-eight years (John 5:1-13), and fed a crowd of five thousand people with a kid's bag lunch of bread and fish (John 6:1-15). Jesus walked on water in the middle of a storm to rescue the swamped and frightened disciples (John 6:16-21), healed a man who had been blind his whole life (John 9:1-7), and in the seventh and climactic sign, raised Lazarus from the dead—calling out to him by name, "Lazarus, come out!" and as John understatedly wrote, "the dead man came out" (John 11:38-44). Each of these seven signs revealed the glory of Jesus, the Son of God.

But even after all these signs—and as John later noted, "Jesus did many other signs in the presence of his disciples, which are not written in this book" (John 20:30)—Jesus was not yet done revealing his glory. Remember what Jesus told his mother Mary at the wedding? "My hour has not yet come."

Later in his ministry Jesus experienced intense resistance, to the point of some people wanting him arrested, but as John wrote, "no one laid hands on him, because his hour had not yet come" (John 7:30). This happened again later when Jesus was teaching in the temple but in the same way, "no one arrested him, because his hour had not yet come" (John 8:20).

But eventually Jesus' hour did come.

Five days before his death, right after his triumphal entry into Jerusalem, Jesus told his disciples Andrew and Philip:

> The hour has come for the Son of Man to be glorified. Very truly, I tell you, unless a grain of wheat falls into the earth and dies, it remains just a single grain; but if it dies, it bears much fruit...Now my soul is troubled. And what should I say—'Father, save me from this hour'? No, it is for this reason that I come to this hour (John 12:23-24, 27).

And a few days later at the Last Supper, as John poignantly wrote,

"Jesus knew that his hour had come to depart from this world and go to the Father. Having loved his own who were in the world, he loved them to the end" (John 13:1). And what did Jesus do at the Last Supper? He washed his disciples' feet and then instituted the sacrament of Holy Communion.

And right before Jesus was finally arrested, he prayed, "Father, the hour has come; glorify your Son so that the Son may glorify you" (John 17:1). And a crowd of false accusers and armed soldiers arrived and arrested Jesus and took him into custody. He was falsely accused, beaten, mocked, and sentenced to be crucified.

And although Jesus indeed feared the mountain in the distance, Calvary, he refused to "settle for the path of least resistance." Instead, Jesus gave his life for a world full of hell-bent and bitter hearts. Some dismissed it as a cosmic mistake, but apparently Jesus believed what Lee Ann Womack sang, "Love might be a mistake but it's worth making." And in the same way Jesus addressed his mother at the wedding in Cana, he did so again, this time from the cross—"Woman, here is your son" (John 19:26-27). Jesus was not sure how he was going to feel that Good Friday, but he knew he was going to do it somehow.

And he did.

Jesus' death on the cross on Good Friday remains the ultimate demonstration of the glory of God. Jesus atoned for the sins of the world, including yours, and demonstrated once and for all that God is a God of love, that as scripture tells us, "God proves his love for us in that while we were still sinners Christ died for us" (Romans 5:8).

And on Easter morning something else unexpected happened as Jesus was raised from the dead, and revealed his glory yet again as the One who not only changes water into wine but also changes death into life.

Back for just a moment to the father/daughter wedding dance

of Jim and Mary Bourne Roberts… Just twelve days after that beautiful dance with his daughter, the hour came for Jim Roberts, and he passed away. And one day the hour will come for each of you as well. It may be on a windy Wednesday afternoon or a frigid Friday evening or a silent Sunday morning—but your hour will come.

But even the hour of your death will not be your final hour, for as John recorded, Jesus also proclaimed, "Very truly, I tell you… the hour is coming when all who are in their graves will hear [my] voice and will come out" (John 5:25, 28). In other words, what happened for Lazarus will happen for Jim Roberts…and will happen for you. What an hour that will be!

Jesus Christ, the One who changes water into wine, changes death into life, and changes hell-bent and bitter hearts with love.

And Jesus always saves the best for last.

Amen.

Very Real Spiritual Hope

When he came to Nazareth, where he had been brought up, he went to the synagogue on the sabbath day, as was his custom. He stood up to read, and the scroll of the prophet Isaiah was given to him. He unrolled the scroll and found the place where it was written: "The Spirit of the Lord is upon me, because he has anointed me to bring good news to the poor. He has sent me to proclaim release to the captives and recovery of sight to the blind, to let the oppressed go free, to proclaim the year of the Lord's favor." And he rolled up the scroll, gave it back to the attendant, and sat down. The eyes of all in the synagogue were fixed on him. Then he began to say to them, "Today this scripture has been fulfilled in your hearing" (Luke 4:16-21).

In the Name of the Father, Son, and Holy Spirit.

In 2004, the iconic singer-songwriter Bob Dylan published a memoir entitled *Chronicles: Volume One*. I read it the week it was published. It is amazing. Since almost fifteen years have elapsed and there is still no second volume, I reread it. As some of you may know, when Bob Dylan was a young man he left his hometown of Hibbing, Minnesota and moved to New York City. While there he frequently went to Morristown, New Jersey, to visit his idol, the legendary folk singer Woody Guthrie, at Greystone Park Psychiatric Hospital, which Dylan described this way:

> The place was really an asylum with no spiritual hope of any kind. Wailing could be heard in the hallways. Most of the patients wore ill-fitting striped uniforms and they would file in and out walking aimlessly about while I played Woody Guthrie songs. One guy's head would be constantly falling forward on his knees. Then he'd raise up and he would fall forward again. Another guy thought he was being chased by spiders and twirled in circles, hands slapping his arms and legs. Someone else who imagined he was president wore an Uncle Sam hat. Patients rolled their eyes, tongues, sniffed the air. One guy continually licking his lips… The scene was frightful (99).

Doubtless one of the Woody Guthrie songs Dylan sang to him was a song I remember singing frequently at school assemblies when I was in first grade:

> This land is your land, this land is my land
> From California to the New York island
> From the Redwood Forest to the Gulf Stream waters
> This land was made for you and me…
> I roamed and I rambled and I followed my footsteps
> To the sparkling sands of her diamond deserts
> While all around me a voice was sounding
> This land was made for you and me

Many years later, in the late 80s, Bob Dylan was performing in Switzerland and in the middle of the concert experienced something else very frightful:

> It all fell apart. For an instant I fell into a black hole. The stage was outdoors and the wind was blowing gales, the kind of night that can blow everything away. I opened my mouth to sing…and nothing came out. The techniques weren't working. I couldn't believe it….There's no pleasure in getting caught in a

situation like this. You can get a panic attack. You're in front of thirty thousand people and they're staring at you and nothing is coming out (153).

The world we live in today can sometimes resemble the psychiatric hospital Dylan visited in New Jersey over fifty years ago, a world that without the gospel is indeed a place "with no spiritual hope of any kind." Moreover, in our own ways many of us find ourselves "walking aimlessly" through our daily duties and responsibilities or twirling in circles slapping at the metaphorical spiders that are not just figments of our imagination. Or like Dylan later experienced, when we least expect it, in some way things can suddenly all fall apart and you fall into a black hole, which can be scary even if it is not in front of thirty thousand people.

Single people who wish they were married, or married people who wish they were single, workers who finally got the promotion they wanted only to wonder if the accompanying drama is worth it, college professors juggling the pressures of being published and attaining tenure and managing an ever-increasing load of administrative institutional busywork while teaching students many of whom would rather stare at their phones than listen to them—all need spiritual hope.

College students who were told over and over again that college would be some of the best years of their life only to be overwhelmed by the pressure of classes and wounded by the false promises of freedom and pleasure and empowerment in a hook-up culture that can leave them feeling used and alone and lost, parents who wish they could connect better with their kids and kids who wish they could measure up to their parents' expectations, middle-aged who are feel trapped in their jobs and are counting down the months to retirement, the elderly in nursing homes watching *The Price is Right* and *Jeopardy* and wondering if they actually made any real difference with their lives—all need spiritual hope.

Regardless of how smart or witty or rich or powerful or beautiful or accomplished you are, there can still be moments when you realize that in spite of all the trappings and accessories and distractions the world offers, without the gospel there is "no spiritual hope of any kind." When things suddenly fall apart, look out.

Today's passage from the Gospel According to Luke recounts the beginning of Jesus's earthly ministry. Jesus had already been baptized in the Jordan River and proclaimed by God the Father as his Beloved Son and filled with the Holy Spirit, symbolized by the descending of a dove from the heavens. Jesus had already been tempted in the wilderness for forty days. Luke tells us that Jesus, "filled with the power of the Spirit, returned to Galilee" (Luke 4:14) and this was followed by a very significant moment in the synagogue:

> When he came to Nazareth, where he had been brought up, he went to the synagogue on the sabbath day, as was his custom. He stood up to read, and the scroll of the prophet Isaiah was given to him. He unrolled the scroll and found the place where it was written: "The Spirit of the Lord is upon me, because he has anointed me to bring good news to the poor. He has sent me to proclaim release to the captives and recovery of sight to the blind, to let the oppressed go free, to proclaim the year of the Lord's favor." And he rolled up the scroll, gave it back to the attendant, and sat down. The eyes of all in the synagogue were fixed on him. Then he began to say to them, "Today this scripture has been fulfilled in your hearing" (Luke 4:16-21).

If Jesus had a mic in the synagogue that day, it would have been the perfect moment for a mic drop. Jesus had revealed why he left heaven to come to earth, and why he became incarnate in a fallen world "with no spiritual hope of any kind." He had also revealed what he would do the next three years as he roamed and rambled and followed his footsteps around Jerusalem, Judea, and Galilee.

Jesus came to offer very real spiritual hope.

Jesus had read in the synagogue, "The Spirit of the Lord has anointed me…to bring good news to the poor." The truth is we are all poor, especially those of us who appear to "have it all." One of the many rock artists heavily influenced by Bob Dylan is Bruce Springsteen, who put it this way on an album that was unjustly shredded by music critics:

> Well I sought gold and diamond rings
> My own drug to ease the pain that living brings
> Walked to the mountain to the valley floor
> Searching for my beautiful reward…
> From a house on a hill a sacred light shines
> I walk through these rooms but none of them are mine
> Down empty hallways I went from door to door
> Searching for my beautiful reward
> Searching for my beautiful reward
> (From his 1992 album *Lucky Town*)

And what good news does Jesus bring to the poor searching "door to door" for their "beautiful reward"? That you are fully known, fully forgiven, fully loved by the One who created you and redeemed you and assures you eternal life—that God's mercies for you are new every morning, that when you feel most alone you are not alone at all, that in spite of all the ways your heart has been broken God offers healing and a new start and what the fourth episode of the *Star Wars* saga calls "a new hope."

Jesus kept reading, "He has sent me to proclaim release to the captives and recovery of sight to the blind, to let the oppressed go free." The same God who in the Old Testament released the captive Israelites from four centuries of slavery in Egypt and "let the oppressed go free," in the New Testament healed a man who had been lame for nearly forty years, healed a man who was paralyzed, straightened the back of an old woman who could not walk without staring at the ground, opened the eyes of a man who had been blind his entire life and had never seen the light of day or anything else, released a woman caught in adultery—"neither do I condemn you"—and even called forth Lazarus from the grave. Jesus put it this way: "Very truly, I tell you, everyone who commits sin is a slave to sin…[but] if the Son makes you free, you will be free indeed" (John 8:34, 36).

Finally, Jesus read that he came "to proclaim the year of the Lord's favor" or what we could call "the year of grace" because that is exactly what "the Lord's favor" is, grace—God's unconditional, one-way love for you that never changes or fades or goes away, God's never changing love for an ever-changing world, and for you.

Jesus read all these things that day in the synagogue, and as the stunned crowd stared at him in silence, he sat down and concluded, "Today this scripture has been fulfilled in your hearing." And for the next three years during Jesus' earthly ministry he did every one of those things, all pointing to what he would do in his suffering and death on Good Friday.

On Good Friday Jesus, who had brought "good news to the poor" himself became poor, and was stripped of all he owned, even his clothes, and led out to die between two broke and broken thieves.

On Good Friday Jesus, who had been sent "to proclaim release to the captives" and "to let the oppressed go free" was himself taken captive by the religious authorities and oppressed by the Roman soldiers, and sentenced to death.

On Good Friday Jesus, who had again and again given "recovery of sight to the blind" was himself blindfolded and struck on the face again and again by his captors who mocked him, "Prophesy! Who is it that struck you?" (Luke 22:64).

And on Good Friday, even after being nailed to the cross,

Jesus proclaimed "the year of the Lord's favor" when he prayed, "Father, forgive them; for they do not know what they are doing" (Luke 23:34).

Back to Bob Dylan and his frightful night on stage in Switzerland…in the same way he had unexpectedly experienced it all falling apart and his falling into a black hole, he suddenly experienced a moment of grace, as he recalls:

> Everything came back, and it came back in multidimension. Even I was surprised. It left me kind of shaky. Immediately, I was flying high… Nobody would have noticed that a metamorphosis had taken place… It was like I'd become a new performer (153).

And Bob Dylan has not stopped performing in the thirty years since that night.

Jesus offered very real spiritual hope that day in the synagogue, and he still does. As you continue to roam and ramble and follow your footsteps, even if it all falls apart and you fall into a black hole, the One who made this land for you and me is still with you, to offer very real spiritual hope.

Amen.

In Fact Christ Has Been Raised from the Dead

Now if Christ is proclaimed as raised from the dead, how can some of you say there is no resurrection of the dead? If there is no resurrection of the dead, then Christ has not been raised; and if Christ has not been raised, then our proclamation has been in vain and your faith has been in vain. We are even found to be misrepresenting God, because we testified of God that he raised Christ—whom he did not raise if it is true that the dead are not raised. For if the dead are not raised, then Christ has not been raised. If Christ has not been raised, your faith is futile and you are still in your sins. Then those also who have died in Christ have perished. If for this life only we have hoped in Christ, we are of all people most to be pitied. But in fact Christ has been raised from the dead, the first fruits of those who have died (1 Corinthians 15:12-20).

In the Name of the Father, Son, and Holy Spirit.

In 2002 the London-based daily newspaper *The Telegraph* published an article that disturbed many people—an article entitled "One Third of Clergy Do Not Believe in the Resurrection." The article was based on extensive research conducted among clergy of the Church of England:

A third of Church of England clergy doubt or

disbelieve in the physical resurrection... While it has long been known that numerous clerics are dubious about the historic creeds of the Church, the survey is the first to disclose how widespread is the skepticism... Doubts are even greater among members of the Modern Churchpeople's Union...only a quarter believe in the physical resurrection and just eight percent in the Virgin Birth.

In this article, one priest put it this way: "There are clearly two churches operating in the Church of England: the believing Church, and the disbelieving Church, and that is a scandal" (Jonathan Petre, July 31, 2002). I wish I could tell you that it is different among clergy in the Episcopal Church, but based on numerous interactions and conversations over the years, that is only a wish. In his 1994 book *Resurrection: Myth or Reality?*, Retired Episcopal Bishop John Shelby Spong dismissed the resurrection this way:

> If the resurrection of Jesus cannot be believed except by assenting to the fantastic descriptions included in the Gospels, then Christianity is doomed. For that view of resurrection is not believable, and if that is all there is, then Christianity which depends upon the truth and authenticity of Jesus' resurrection, is also not believable (238).

And of course such skepticism regarding the resurrection extends beyond those who are not part of the Modern Churchpeople's Union (sounds like a fun group, doesn't it?) or disbelieving Anglican clergy and bishops. Last decade several acclaimed writers advocated what became known as the New Atheism movement.

The late British writer Christopher Hitchens was part of this group and the author of the 2007 book *God Is Not Great*. He once quipped on Instagram, "Do I think I'm going to paradise? Of course not. I wouldn't go if I was asked. I don't want to live in some celestial North Korea for one thing, where all I get to do is praise the Dear Leader from dawn till dusk." Fellow New Atheist writer Sam Harris, in his 2004 book *The End of Faith*, blasphemously summed up Jesus Christ and Holy Communion this way, "Jesus Christ—who as it turns out was born of a virgin, cheated death, and rose bodily into the heavens— can now be eaten in the form of a cracker. A few Latin words spoken over your favorite Burgundy, and you can drink his blood as well" (*The New York Times*, September 5, 2004). I hope those quotes make you uncomfortable. Both Hitchens' and Harris' books remained on *The New York Times Bestsellers* list for many weeks.

And yet resurrection—the resurrection of Jesus Christ and the resurrection of the dead—is at the heart of the Christian faith. The brilliant theologian J. I. Packer, who has taught and written about Christian theology for nearly seventy years, wrote this in the 1987 book *Did Jesus Rise from the Dead?*:

> Non-Christian faiths have an inner structure different from Christianity… They offer ultimate happiness, however they conceive it, as a prize to be gained from God, or the gods, or the cosmic order, through knowledgeable and worthy action on our part… But Christianity, which sees ultimate happiness as rescue from sin and an unending love relationship with one's Creator, offers this salvation package as a gift, to be received here and now by admitting our helplessness and entering into a faith relationship with Jesus Christ, the divine-human Savor and Lord (143).

Packer then hones in on the centrality of the resurrection in the Christian faith:

> When Christians are asked to make good their claim that this scheme is truth, they point to Jesus' Resurrection. The Easter event, so they affirm, demonstrated Jesus' deity; validated his teaching; attested the completion of his work of atonement

for sin; confirms his present cosmic dominion and his coming reappearance as Judge; assures us that his personal pardon, presence, and power in people's lives today is fact; and guarantees each believer's own re-embodiment by Resurrection in the world to come (143).

In the New Testament the Apostle Paul, before his conversion to Christianity, waged angry persecution against the Christian Church, persecution that was even more angry and blasphemous than anything Christopher Hitchens or Sam Harris ever wrote. Paul initially considered Jesus an imposter, a charlatan, and dismissed his death on the cross as a good thing and his resurrection as a hoax. In his First Letter to Timothy, Paul described the type of person he was before his conversion: "I was formerly a blasphemer, a persecutor, and a man of violence" (1 Timothy 1:13). But Paul, on his way to Damascus in order to persecute the Christians there, encountered none other than the Resurrected Jesus. Scripture tells us:

> Now as he was going along and approaching Damascus, suddenly a light from heaven flashed around him. He fell to the ground and heard a voice saying to him, "Why do you persecute me?" He asked, "Who are you, Lord?" The reply came, "I am Jesus, whom you are persecuting. But get up and enter the city, and you will be told what to do" (Acts 9:3-6).

Paul, who had mocked and persecuted Christians, even to the point of condemning them to death, personally encountered the Resurrected Jesus, who did not rebuke Paul for his blasphemous unbelief, but gave him grace instead, as Paul later described it, again to his protégé Timothy:

> I received mercy because I had acted ignorantly in unbelief, and the grace of our Lord overflowed for me with the faith and love that are in Christ Jesus. The saying is sure and worthy of full acceptance, that

Christ Jesus came into the world to save sinners—of whom I am the foremost (1 Timothy 1:13-15).

The grace Paul received from the Resurrected Jesus changed the course of his life, and he went on to plant many Christian churches in Europe and Asia Minor and to write thirteen of the twenty-seven books of the New Testament.

One of those churches was the church in Corinth, and one of those letters his First Letter to the Corinthians, in which he emphasized the gospel as being the most important thing in the world: "I handed on to you as of first importance…that Christ died for our sins in accordance with the scriptures, and that he was buried, and that he was raised on the third day in accordance with the scriptures" and then Paul added, "he appeared also to me" (1 Corinthians 15:3-4, 8). In today's passage, Paul is crystal clear about to the centrality of resurrection in the Christian faith:

> Now if Christ is proclaimed as raised from the dead, how can some of you say there is no resurrection of the dead? If there is no resurrection of the dead, then Christ has not been raised; and if Christ has not been raised, then our proclamation has been in vain and your faith has been in vain. We are even found to be misrepresenting God, because we testified of God that he raised Christ—whom he did not raise if it is true that the dead are not raised. For if the dead are not raised, then Christ has not been raised. If Christ has not been raised, your faith is futile and you are still in your sins. Then those also who have died in Christ have perished. If for this life only we have hoped in Christ, we are of all people most to be pitied. But in fact Christ has been raised from the dead, the first fruits of those who have died (1 Corinthians 15:12-20).

Paul wrote about the reality of the physical resurrection of Christ and the reality of the resurrection of the dead. There is nothing metaphorical or figurative in this passage. It is high octane gospel full of high octane hope. Resurrection is central to Christianity because resurrection is central to the identity of Christ himself, who proclaimed, "I am the resurrection and the life" (John 11:25). And as Paul wrote, indeed "Christ Jesus came into the world to save sinners," and on the cross "the grace of our Lord overflowed" for the Apostle Paul, and for Bishop Spong, and for Christopher Hitchens, and for Sam Harris, and for the believing church, and for the disbelieving church…and for you.

Leo Tolstoy's 1886 novella, *The Death of Ivan Ilyich*, recounts the death of a judge in nineteenth century Russia. As his final hour on earth rapidly approaches Ivan Ilyich assesses his life, and when his final hour arrives, it arrives with hope:

> "And death? Where is it?" [Ivan Ilyich] searched for his accustomed fear of death and could not find it. Where was death? What death? There was no fear because there was no death. Instead of death there was light. "So that's it!" he exclaimed. "What bliss!" All this happened in a single moment, but the significance of that moment was lasting…"It is all over," said someone standing beside him. He heard these words and repeated them in his soul. "Death is over," he said to himself. "There is no more death." He drew in a breath, broke off in the middle of it, stretched himself out, and died (Bantam classic edition 133-134).

And who do you think was there at the final earthly moment of Ivan Ilyich? Who do you think was there to take away his fear of death? Who do you think was there to give him light? Who do you think was there to inspire him to exclaim, "What bliss!" The same One who encountered Paul on the road to Damascus—the Resurrected Jesus, the Resurrection and the Life.

"In fact Christ has been raised from the dead, the first fruits of those who have died." The fruits of those who have died will include you, as scripture also states, "If the Spirit of him who raised Jesus from the dead dwells in you, he who raised Christ from the dead will give life to your mortal bodies also" (Romans 8:11).

One more illustration… One day during English class in my senior year of high school, I was first exposed to "Holy Sonnet 10," one of the most famous poems of the great early seventeenth century Anglican priest and poet John Donne (1572-1631)—a poem about the Christian hope of the resurrection that really moved me that day, and still does these many years later:

> Death be not proud, though some have called thee
> Mighty and dreadful, for, thou art not so,
> For, those, whom thou think'st, thou dost overthrow,
> Die not, poor death, nor yet canst thou kill me;
> From rest and sleep, which but thy pictures be,
> Much pleasure, then from thee, much more must flow,
> And soonest out best men with thee do go,
> Rest of their bones, and soul's delivery.
> Thou art slave to fate, chance, war, and sickness dwell,
> And poppy, or charms, can make us sleep as well,
> And better than thy stroke; why swell'st thou then?
> One short sleep past, we wake eternally,
> And death shall be no more, Death thou shalt die.

"In fact Christ has been raised from the dead." That is the good news of the gospel. And today the Resurrected Jesus beckons you to receive anew the same grace he gave to the Apostle Paul, grace that changes angry, blasphemous disbelief into faith and hope and love.

Amen.

No Myth at All

Now the Lord is the Spirit, and where the Spirit of the Lord is, there is freedom (2 Corinthians 3:17).

In the Name of the Father, Son, and Holy Spirit.
    Each of us is born with a yearning for our idea of freedom. We chafe against rules of any kind. We are never taught this; it is hardwired into our human DNA. Think about it. When you were young if you were told not to take a cookie out of the cookie jar on the kitchen counter, what was the very first thing, the only thing, you wanted to do? Take a cookie from the cookie jar, hopefully when your parents were not looking. In elementary school when your class was walking to lunch or recess and your teacher would yell, "No running in the hallways!" what was the very first thing, the only thing, you wanted to do? Run in the hallway. When you are a kid, hallways literally beckon you to run—run you must, run you do.
    We do not like rules. When I was in fourth grade, my friends and I were discussing how annoying rules were in sports, how rules spoiled all the fun. "Wouldn't it better if there were no rules?" we thought. "Wouldn't it be much more fun?" So we put our theory into practice and decided that the next day at recess we would play a new game we invented called "No Rules Football" (I am not

making this up). And so we did. The next morning at recess we gathered at the school field with a football, divided into two teams and began playing "No Rules Football," which we thought would be so much fun, so awesome, because who needs rules?

As you can imagine within a few minutes arguments broke out about what was inbounds or out of bounds because there were no rules and therefore no sidelines. Arguments broke out about how many yards yielded a first down because there were no rules and therefore who were you to say how many yards were needed for a first down? Arguments broke out about pass interference as kids were tackled before they could even get open because there were no rules and therefore no such thing as pass interference. Arguments broke out about everything you could imagine and pretty soon our amazing game of "No Rules Football" devolved into utter chaos and not a few fistfights. We all ended up having to sit out recess for the rest of the week. Needless to say, we returned to "regular" football the next week.

And lest you think that is all just silly, read the 1954 novel *Lord of the Flies* by William Golding. Our idea of freedom, our idea or either not having rules at all or making our own rules often leads to chaos and destruction. And this persists into adulthood. As adults there are several myths about freedom that can end up being much more destructive to our lives than "No Rules Football."

One is the myth of financial freedom. You will have financial freedom when you have enough money, right? If you earn more money, have all your insurance policies in order, retire the mortgage on your house, maintain and grow all your pension and IRA accounts to a certain level, have a large and diverse investment portfolio, have at least six months' worth of living expenses in a "rainy day account," you will achieve financial freedom, right?

Now please do not mishear me...all those things are good in and of themselves, and certainly sound financial practices are beneficial—you know this—but the idea of financial freedom itself is a myth because, for human beings, enough is never enough. Jesus put it this way: "Be on your guard against all kinds of greed; for one's life does not consist in the abundance of possessions" (Luke 12:15). Then Jesus told a parable to illustrate this:

> The land of a rich man produced abundantly. And he thought to himself, "What should I do, for I have no place to store my crops?" Then he said, "I will do this: I will pull down my barns and build larger ones, and there I will store all my grain and my goods. And I will say to my soul, 'Soul, you have ample goods laid up for many years; relax, eat, drink, be merry.'" But God said to him, "You fool! This very night your life is being demanded of you. And the things you have prepared, whose will they be?" So it is with those who store up treasures for themselves but are not rich toward God (Luke 12:16-21).

You may remember what billionaire John D. Rockefeller said when asked, "How much money is enough money?" "Just a little bit more," he replied. You would think being a billionaire would give you financial freedom—but apparently not. Scripture warns, "Those who want to be rich fall into temptation and are trapped by many senseless and harmful desires that plunge people into ruin and destruction" (1 Timothy 6:9). Financial freedom is a myth.

A second myth about freedom is the myth of sexual freedom. (Let's get really uncomfortable for a moment). The sexual revolution was ushered in during the 1960s and has continued unabated to the present as any talk about any guidelines or restrictions or taboos about human sexuality is dismissed and rejected out of hand, as anyone anytime should be free to express themselves sexually as they deem fit. Who are you or anybody else to say or think anything that in any way undermines sexual freedom? But when it comes to the human heart regarding sexuality, just like money, enough is never enough. The pursuit of fifty shades of whatever continues…but in its wake are the flotsam and jetsam of unspeakable hurt, wrecked marriages, various forms of sexual addiction, and of course rampant venereal disease—damaged hearts, damaged lives. Where is the freedom in that?

A third myth about freedom is the myth of freedom coming from being your own boss. A few years ago, CNBC published an online article entitled "'Being Your Own Boss' is One of the Biggest Myths of Entrepreneurship" that stated:

> Anytime you talk to a current entrepreneur or even someone thinking about starting their own business, usually one of the biggest motivations is wanting to be their own boss. The idea of "working for the man" has lost its luster, and the pursuit of freedom to do what you want, when you want is extremely sexy and appealing. However, getting to be your own boss is one of the biggest myths about entrepreneurship. First, one of the most important assets of a company is its customers. If you have no customers—or more accurately, no paying customers—you have no business. It is impossible to have a business without any customers. This gives your customers the ultimate power—basically, they own you. So, if you believe owning a business means that you get to be the boss, forget it; the customer is the number one boss, bar none (September 28, 2016).

I once was at a lunch table at a clergy conference listening to a young priest who was chafing about being an assistant priest and whining about wanting to be a rector so he could "be his own boss." I chuckled inside and thought, "You have much to learn, young grasshopper." The ordination to the priesthood vows in *The Book of Common Prayer* state, "You are to love and serve the people among whom you work, caring alike for young and old, strong and weak, rich and poor" (531). There is nothing in there about the freedom of being your own boss.

So you may be wondering, "Where are you going with this sermon? Why are you talking about the myth of financial freedom, and the myth of sexual freedom, and the myth of freedom from being your own boss?" Because when it comes to the gospel, there is freedom that is no myth at all, as Paul wrote in today's passage from his Second Letter to the Corinthians, "Now the Lord is the Spirit, and where the Spirit of the Lord is, there is freedom" (2 Corinthians 3:17). Where the Spirit of the Lord is, there is freedom.

At the outset of his earthly ministry Jesus, after being baptized in the Jordan and subsequently enduring forty days of temptation in the wilderness, arose in a synagogue and read these words from Isaiah, "The Spirit of the Lord is upon me, because he has anointed me to proclaim release to the captives…to let the oppressed go free" (Luke 4:18).

This kind of freedom is not something we can create for ourselves; it is a gift from the Holy Spirit—"Where the Spirit of the Lord is, there is freedom." Throughout his earthly ministry Jesus did exactly what Isaiah had prophesied as he proclaimed release to those taken captive by their own efforts to achieve freedom. To those who sought financial freedom through wealth only to find themselves enslaved to it, he proclaimed, "Go, sell your possessions, and give the money to the poor, and you will have treasure in heaven; then come, follow me" (Matthew 19:21) and "It is more blessed to give than to receive" (Acts 20:35).

I recently came across a story of what this looks like. A waitress, seven months pregnant with her first child, was working at the Lamp Post Diner in Gloucester Township, New Jersey. One of her customers was a police officer who was eating lunch alone. The bill totaled $8.75. When she picked up the signed credit card slip on the table she was stunned to see that the police officer had paid

$108.75, giving her a tip of $100. Underneath this ridiculously generous tip was written, "Enjoy your first [child]. You will never forget it." The waitress's father, Brian Cadigan, posted the following thank-you note about it on Facebook: "What a wonderful person to not only leave a VERY generous tip, but a lovely message. I don't know you, Mr. Police Officer, but you made my little girl cry, and made her year. Thank you. I always had the utmost respect for Officers, but you went above and beyond not just being an officer but a beautiful human being. God bless." The officer insists on remaining anonymous. True financial freedom looks like that.

To those who sought sexual freedom through sexual license only to find themselves in trouble or victimized Jesus proclaimed, "Neither do I condemn thee; go and sin no more" (John 8:11, KJV). Jesus gave forgiveness and grace.

And to those who sought freedom from being their own boss only to find themselves enslaved to their own lust for power, Jesus proclaimed, "Whoever wishes to become great among you must be your servant, and whoever wishes to be first among you must be slave to all. For the Son of Man came not to be served but to serve, and to give his life a ransom for many" (Mark 10:43-45). In other words, Jesus taught in word and action the truth of what we pray in The Collect for Peace in *The Book of Common Prayer*—that true freedom comes not in serving ourselves, but in serving God, "whose service is perfect freedom" (57). As Jesus taught in what became known as The Lord's Prayer true freedom is found in "Thy kingdom come," not "my kingdom come"—true freedom is found in "Thy will be done," not "my will be done."

Jesus proclaimed "release to the captives" and "let the oppressed go free" to those who sought the myth of financial freedom, or the myth of sexual freedom, or the myth of freedom from being your own boss—because Jesus was anointed with the Holy Spirit and "where the Spirit of the Lord is, there is freedom," because as Jesus said, "If the Son makes you free, you will be free indeed" (John 8:36).

And on Good Friday, Jesus used his freedom as the Son of God to give his life in your place, to set you free from the cages you have created for yourself in your own futile efforts to achieve your idea freedom, to show a world of "no rules football" what the single rule of love looks like.

The gospel is good news for those who have learned the hard way what Kris Kristofferson wrote and Janis Joplin famously sang: "Freedom's just another word for nothin' left to lose" (from "Me and Bobby McGee").

The gospel is good news for those who have been burned by the myths of financial freedom or sexual freedom or freedom from being your own boss, because "Where the Spirit of the Lord is there is freedom."

And that kind of freedom is no myth at all.

Amen.

New and Contrite Hearts

Ash Wednesday

Create in me a clean heart, O God, and renew a right spirit within me (Psalm 51:11, BCP 657).

In the Name of the Father, Son, and Holy Spirit.

The other day I was walking out of Walmart and saw one of my favorite things in the world—a table where Girl Scout cookies were being sold, one of the best things about March. As I bought some of their legendary Thin Mint cookies I had an unexpected and troubling flashback to a year when I gave up chocolate for Lent without taking into account Girl Scout Thin Mint Cookies… probably the longest season of Lent in my life. Whatever you give up for Lent, don't ever do that…

In 2014, my daughter Cate and I spent a week in England, including a couple days in London. We spent one morning visiting the famous (and infamous) Tower of London—or as it is officially called: Her Majesty's Royal Palace and Fortress of the Tower of London. It was founded by none other than William the Conqueror following the 1066 Norman Conquest. The Tower of London is a microcosm of British national life. It has served as a treasury, an armory, and a mint. It even housed the royal menagerie during the Middle Ages. It has an ornate chapel, where centuries of prayers and services of Holy Communion have occurred. It also houses the famous crown jewels, all 23,578 gemstones.

And of course, the Tower of London has also served as notorious prison, where many famous people were held, not just criminals, but those labeled as religious heretics, including the writer of the English Prayer Book and the leading figure of the English Reformation, Archbishop Thomas Cranmer (1489-1556). We saw the huge iron gate, the so-called Traitor's Gate, through which Cranmer was brought across the moat into the Tower of London in 1553 at the age of 64.

We saw the spot where, also in 1553, sixteen-year-old Lady Jane Grey was beheaded after her nine-day reign as queen. And we saw the frightening cells where prisoners were confined, and the even more frightening torture chambers where victims were stretched on the rack and endured unspeakable pain and agony. All of this occurred at the Tower of London. The amount of history that has unfolded there over nearly a millennium is simply overwhelming.

And later that night as I lay awake I kept thinking about the Tower of London, and something very sobering, very poignant occurred to me. The Tower of London was just like my heart inasmuch that my heart is a microcosm of my life. My heart has a treasury and a mint, and houses the crown jewels of my life, where I cherish memories that are the most important to me—where I hold dear those closest to me, those still alive and those who have died. My heart has a chapel, where I thank God every day, where I pray every day for my family, for the church, for the needs in our lives—some of those prayers transcending words.

But in the same way that there are also dark and frightening places in the Tower of London, there are also dark and frightening places in my heart. I wish this was not the case, but it is. My heart

A Collection of Sermons

has its own prison cells where I may hold grudges against others, others against whom I may at times wish to use the weapons I store in my heart's armory. My heart has its own torture chambers where I may stretch myself on the rack of regret, or wish I could stretch the impossibly difficult and challenging or just plain mean people in my life. My heart has a chopping block where some of the little or not so little deaths in my heart have taken place.

Perhaps you can relate. Perhaps your heart is also like the Tower of London.

In addition to our hearts having beautiful places as well as dark and frightening places, our hearts are also often hard. Scripture often speaks of the danger of having a hard heart (Mark 8:17; Romans 2:5, etc.). My years of personal and pastoral experience have taught me that often hard hearts are directly connected to deep hurts—the deeper the hurt, the harder the heart. Along these lines, in 1981 the band Quarterflash had their biggest hit that put it this way:

> Cryin' on the corner, waitin' in the rain
> I swear I'll never ever wait again
> You gave me your word, but words for you are lies
> Darlin', in my wildest dreams, I never thought I'd go
> But it's time to let you know
> I'm gonna harden my heart
> I'm gonna swallow my tears
> I'm gonna turn and leave you here
> (From their song "Harden My Heart" on their eponymous debut album)

During the season of Lent, we are invited to examine our hearts, or rather to ask God to examine our hearts—as the psalmist wrote, "Search me out, O God, and know my heart; try me and know my restless thoughts" (Psalm 139:22, *BCP* 795). This is serious business, because what happens in our hearts impacts *everything* in our lives, and more importantly, *everyone* in our lives. Scripture tells us, "Keep your heart with all vigilance, for from it flow the springs of life" (Proverbs 4:23). The "springs of life" that flow from your heart make an impact—whether those "springs of life" are full of love and gratitude, or full of anger and bitterness.

The season of Lent is a season about the heart.

Along these lines, what is the one petition in the collect for Ash Wednesday? "Create and make in us new and contrite hearts." Why? So as we continue in the collect, "that we, worthily lamenting our sins and acknowledging our wretchedness, may obtain of you, the God of all mercy, perfect remission and forgiveness" (BCP 264). That is what Lent is all about.

Scripture does not mince words when it comes to describing the reality of the condition of the human heart. The Old Testament prophet Jeremiah, whose ministry took place about six centuries before Christ, wrote, "The heart is devious above all else—who can understand it?" (Jeremiah 17:9). Jesus goes even further: "Out of the heart come evil intentions, murder, adultery, fornication, theft, false witness, slander" (Matthew 15:19).

King David experienced the reality of this. King David, whom scripture identifies as "a man after [God's] own heart" (1 Samuel 13:14; Acts 13:22) succumbed to the dark and frightening places in his heart and committed adultery with Bathsheba and then after learning she was pregnant with his child, conspired to have her husband Uriah, who had been one of David's personal right hand warriors, to be abandoned and killed in battle. Unbeknownst to him, Uriah actually hand delivered King David's conspiring letter to Joab, the letter that meant his death.

King David thought he had covered up all his tracks, but God knew what he did, and sent Nathan the prophet to confront him. As a result, David repented, and wrote Psalm 51, the psalm we pray together every year on Ash Wednesday, the psalm in which we ask

God for the same thing we ask in the Collect for Ash Wednesday: "Create in me a clean heart, O God" (Psalm 51:11, *BCP* 266).

Moreover, during the "Litany of Penitence" in *The Book of Common Prayer*, a litany we also pray every year on Ash Wednesday, the first thing we confess is: "We have not loved you with our whole heart, and mind, and strength. We have not loved our neighbors as ourselves. We have not forgiven others, as we have been forgiven" (*BCP* 267). During the entire rest of the "Litany of Penitence" we confess various ways that lack of love and lack of forgiveness impact everything and everyone in our lives. There is nothing esoteric or obscure or arcane about any of this. This is all real life. It all boils down to love and forgiveness. It is all goes back to our need for God to "create in us new and contrite hearts."

And at the end of the "Litany of Penitence," we appeal to the one thing, the only thing that can "create in us new and contrite hearts": the love of God in Jesus Christ, specifically in his death and resurrection—"Accomplish in us the work of your salvation," we pray, "that we may show forth your glory in the world. By the cross and passion and your Son our Lord, bring us with all your saints to the joy of his resurrection" (*BCP* 268-269). Only the love of God can create in us new and contrite hearts. Only the love of God can replace our hard hearts with new and contrite hearts. Only the love God can heal the deepest hurts in our hearts.

On Good Friday Jesus died of a broken heart in order to "create in us new and contrite hearts." After his death Jesus was pierced by a soldier's lance in that same sacred heart, and as blood and water sprang forth, the "spring of life" of God's love and forgiveness sprang forth for every hard heart in the world, including yours.

In 1543, ten years before being imprisoned in the Tower of London, Archbishop Thomas Cranmer beautifully described how "new and contrite hearts" created by the love of God enable us in turn to share that love with others: "If the profession of our faith of the remission of our own sins enter within us into the deepness of our hearts, then it must kindle a warm fire of love in our hearts towards God, and towards all others for the love of God" (*Thomas Cranmer's Doctrine of Repentance* 185). Love begets love. That is the fruit of the gospel.

So during Lent may God, who will never "turn and leave you here," do just that—create a new and contrite heart in you, and heal the deepest hurts in your heart with his "perfect remission and forgiveness" and his unconditional love.

Amen.

Grace in the Wilderness of Temptation

Jesus, full of the Holy Spirit, returned from the Jordan and was led by the Spirit in the wilderness, where for forty days he was tempted by the devil. He ate nothing at all during those days, and when they were over, he was famished. The devil said to him, "If you are the Son of God, command this stone to become a loaf of bread." Jesus answered him, "It is written, 'One does not live by bread alone.'" Then the devil led him up and showed him in an instant all the kingdoms of the world. And the devil said to him, "To you I will give their glory and all this authority; for it has been given over to me, and I give it to anyone I please. If you, then, will worship me, it will all be yours." Jesus answered him, "It is written, 'Worship the Lord your God, and serve only him.'" Then the devil took him to Jerusalem, and placed him on the pinnacle of the temple, saying to him, "If you are the Son of God, throw yourself down from here, for it is written, 'He will command his angels concerning you, to protect you,' and 'On their hands they will bear you up, so that you will not dash your foot against a stone.'" Jesus answered him, "It is said, 'Do not put the Lord your God to the test.'" When the devil had finished every test, he departed from him until an opportune time (Luke 4:1-13).

Grace to Help in Time of Need

In the Name of the Father, Son, and Holy Spirit.

Every year on the First Sunday of Lent the gospel passage is an account of Jesus' temptation in the wilderness. Today I am preaching on how the specific temptations Jesus faced parallel temptations we all face—and how God meets us in the wilderness of temptation with grace. This will include several insights from a gem of a book about Jesus' wilderness temptation entitled *In the Name of Jesus* (1989) by the brilliant late Catholic priest and theologian, Henri Nouwen.

Jesus' temptation in the wilderness immediately followed his anointing as the Messiah at his baptism in the Jordan River. It was part of God's plan as scripture tells us Jesus "was led by the Spirit in the wilderness, where for forty days he was tempted by the devil." Every single one of those forty days Jesus was tempted by the devil, but the specific temptations recorded in scripture took place at the end of these forty days when Jesus was most vulnerable (Luke 4:1-2).

It is often in the aftermath of a major event in our lives—like a graduation or a wedding, or the birth of a child or a job promotion—or after a powerful experience of God in your life—that you are especially vulnerable to temptation. There is truth to the idea that after some kind of "mountaintop" experience with God you need to return to the valley of real life. We certainly acknowledge this liturgically as the gospel passage every year on the Last Sunday of Epiphany is the mountaintop experience of Jesus' Transfiguration, followed the very next Sunday with his temptation in the wilderness of the valley. This is no coincidence.

Similarly, Luke writes that Jesus was "famished"—strong word, not just "hungry" but "famished"— when the devil tempted him in three specific ways: the temptation to turn stones to bread, the temptation of power, and the temptation to put God to the test. The devil waited until Jesus has had his "mountaintop" experience, until Jesus was alone, until Jesus was "famished" before breaking out these "big" temptations. Think about the big temptations in your life for a moment—does any of this sound familiar to your own experience?

The first thing the devil tempted Jesus with was to meet his own needs, specifically his immediate need for food: "If you are the Son of God, command this stone to become a loaf of bread," and "Jesus answered him, 'It is written, One does not live by bread alone'" (Luke 4:3-4). Jesus cites scripture in response to this first temptation, as he will again with the other temptations. Jesus, the incarnate Word of God, stands on scripture, the written word of God, specifically a passage from the Old Testament book of Deuteronomy in which Moses reminded Israel of God's provision of manna when they, just like Jesus, were famished in the wilderness:

> He humbled you by letting you hunger, then by feeding you with manna, with which neither you nor your ancestors were acquainted, in order to make you understand that one does not live by bread alone, but by every word that comes from the mouth of the Lord (Deuteronomy 8:3).

Of course this begs the question, where are you hungry in your life—not just hungry, where are you famished in your life? If you try to fill that hunger by your own power or in a way that you know is wrong, if you try metaphorically to turn stones into bread, you will find yourself in trouble. Only God can fill the places in your life where you are famished—as the brilliant Church Father Augustine wrote in the of the fourth century in his *Confessions*, "You have made us for yourself, and our heart is restless until it finds it rest in you" (Oxford World's Classics edition, 3).

Another way to view this first temptation of turning stones into bread is what Henri Nouwen described in his book *In the Name of Jesus* as "the temptation to be relevant." Listen to this:

> Beneath all the great accomplishments of our time there is a deep current of despair. While efficiency and control are the great aspirations of our society, the loneliness, isolation, lack of friendship and intimacy, broken relationships, boredom, feelings of emptiness and depression, and a deep sense of uselessness fill the hearts of millions of people in our success-oriented world (33).

Nouwen was right thirty years ago, and he is right today. Beware the temptation to fill the areas in your life where you are famished, in your own power in ways you know are wrong, all under the guise of being "relevant."

Then Jesus faced the second temptation, as Luke wrote:

> Then the devil led him up and showed him in an instant all the kingdoms of the world. And the devil said to him, "To you I will give their glory and all this authority; for it has been given over to me, and I will give it to anyone I please. If you, then, will worship me, it will all be yours" (Luke 4:5-7).

Jesus responded to this temptation by again appealing to scripture: "It is written, 'Worship the Lord your God, and serve only him'" (Luke 4:8). This scripture also comes from Deuteronomy, when the Lord through Moses warned Israel about the dangers of idolatry as they prepared to enter the Promised Land: "The Lord your God you shall fear; him you shall serve, and by his name alone you shall swear" (Deuteronomy 6:13).

In short, Jesus was tempted with power—not just a little power, but with power over "all the kingdoms of the world." Think about that. What would you do if you were tempted with that? The temptation to power is particularly wicked because as human beings we love to be in charge, or at least under the illusion that we are in charge. The temptation to power is insidious because there is truth to the maxim, "Power corrupts; absolute power corrupts absolutely." And yet, in his incarnation Jesus had "emptied himself" and set aside his power in order to become not just a human being but a servant (Philippians 2:7), a servant who would eventually give his life "as a ransom for many" (Mark 10:45)—and not even authority over "all the kingdoms of the world" could deviate him from that.

In your life, where are you tempted with power, with the idea that if you were in charge you could make everything better? This temptation can be so enticing that you may find yourself willing to cut "just a few" moral corners, to tell "just a few" white lies, or jettison "just a few" of your beliefs in order to gain that power. Again Henri Nouwen cuts right to the chase:

> What makes the temptation of power so seemingly irresistible? Maybe it is that power offers an easy substitute for the hard task of love. It seems easier to be God than to love God, easier to control people than to love people, easier to own life than to love life… The long painful history of the church is the history of people ever and again tempted to choose power over love (77).

Jesus chose love over power. Jesus did not come to wield power over the world; he came to love the world. Although we may tempted by power, thankfully Jesus was not. I know in my own life every time I chose power over love, even when I "was right," I later regretted it, later wished I had chosen love over power instead.

So the devil tempted Jesus again:

> Then the devil took him on the pinnacle of the temple, saying to him, "If you are the Son of God, throw yourself down from here, for it is written, 'He will command his angels concerning you, to protect you' and 'On their hands they will bear you up, so that you will not dash your foot against a stone'" (Luke 4:9-11).

In this third temptation, the devil throws a particularly wicked curveball because he incorporates scripture, the same word of God written, to which Jesus had appealed. The devil was right in that the psalmist indeed wrote about how God commands angels to watch over us and bear us up so that we "will not dash [our] foot against a stone"—that comes straight from Psalm 91:11-12. But the devil misused the scripture here and tragically history is replete with examples of scripture being misused to justify things that in the overall context of scripture are completely unjustifiable: slavery, bigamy, misogyny, racism, sexism…just to name a few.

And yet, thankfully, Jesus would not yield as he again appealed to scripture: "It is said, 'Do not put the Lord your God to the test'" (Luke 4:12). Again, Jesus appealed to Deuteronomy, when the Lord had warned Israel, "Do not put the Lord your God to the test, as you tested him at Massah" (Deuteronomy 6:16). It was at Massah when the Israelites tested God by demanding Moses to give them water to drink as they, just like Jesus, were in the wilderness.

At God's command Moses struck the rock and water poured out to quench their thirst, but the problem was the underlying premise behind their request as scripture tells us, "Moses called the place Massah (which means "test") and Meribah (which means "quarrel") because the Israelites quarreled and tested the Lord saying, "Is the Lord among us or not?" (Exodus 17:1-7). Again, think about your life for a moment…is there a situation in which you are tempted to test God, a situation in which like the Israelites you are asking, "Is the Lord among us or not?"

The devil tempted Jesus to test God by doing something spectacular, by throwing himself from the pinnacle of the temple so that the angels would catch him. But as Henri Nouwen observes, "Jesus refused to be a stunt man. He did not come to prove himself" (55). Jesus overcame the temptation to put God to the test.

Luke ends his account of Jesus' temptation in the wilderness with the ominous words: "When the devil had finished every test, he departed from [Jesus] until an opportune time" (Luke 4:13)—and that most "opportune time" arrived during Holy Week. On Palm Sunday as the crowds chanted, "Blessed is he who comes in the name of the Lord! Hosanna in the highest!" it would have been the seemingly perfect time for Jesus to turn stones into bread, but he didn't. Instead, in response to those complaining about the chanting crowds Jesus simply said, "I tell you, if these were silent, the stones would shout out" (Luke 19:40).

During his betrayal and arrest it would have been the seemingly perfect time for Jesus to choose power over love, but he didn't. Instead, he chose love over power, as he always did. And during his suffering on the cross it would have been the seemingly perfect time for Jesus to do something spectacular and prove himself, but he didn't. Instead, the only thing Jesus chose to prove was that he loved the world unconditionally, including you, as scripture tells us, "God proved his love for us in that while we still were sinners Christ died for us" (Roman 5:8).

Jesus taught us to pray, "lead us not into temptation" because he knew hard that temptation could be, and that often we cannot or do not overcome it. Instead Jesus, the only one who as ever lived who could, and did, overcome every temptation, offers grace to us when we find ourselves particularly vulnerable to temptation— after a mountaintop experience, or isolated and famished in the wilderness.

Scripture assures us, "We do not have a high priest who is unable to sympathize with our weaknesses, but we have on who in every respect has been [tempted] as we are, yet without sin"—and tells us what to do when we are in the wilderness of temptation, "Let us therefore approach the throne of grace with boldness, so that we may receive mercy and find grace to help in time of need" (Hebrews 4:15-16).

Be encouraged....for God offers grace in the wilderness of temptation.

Amen

The Lord Helps Those Who Cannot Help Themselves

Moses was keeping the flock of his father-in-law Jethro, the priest of Midian; he led his flock beyond the wilderness, and came to Horeb, the mountain of God. There the angel of the Lord appeared to him in a flame of fire out of a bush; he looked, and the bush was blazing, yet it was not consumed. Then Moses said, "I must turn aside and look at this great sight, and see why the bush is not burned up." When the Lord saw that he had turned aside to see, God called to him out of the bush, "Moses, Moses!" And he said, "Here I am." Then he said, "Come no closer! Remove the sandals from your feet, for the place on which you are standing is holy ground." He said further, "I am the God of your father, the God of Abraham, the God of Isaac, and the God of Jacob." And Moses hid his face, for he was afraid to look at God. Then the Lord said, "I have observed the misery of my people who are in Egypt; I have heard their cry on account of their taskmasters. Indeed, I know their sufferings, and I have come down to deliver them from the Egyptians, and to bring them up out of that land to a good and broad land, a land flowing with milk and honey, to the country of the Canaanites, the Hittites, the Amorites, the Perizzites, the Hivites, and the Jebusites. The cry of the Israelites has now come to me; I have also seen how the Egyptians oppress them. So come, I will send you to Pharaoh to bring my people, the Israelites, out of Egypt." But Moses said to God, "Who am I that

I should go to Pharaoh, and bring the Israelites out of Egypt?" He said, "I will be with you; and this shall be the sign for you that it is I who sent you: when you have brought the people out of Egypt, you shall worship God on this mountain." But Moses said to God, "If I come to the Israelites and say to them, 'The God of your ancestors has sent me to you,' and they ask me, 'What is his name?' what shall I say to them?" God said to Moses, "I am who I am." He said further, "Thus you shall say to the Israelites, 'I am' has sent me to you." God also said to Moses, "Thus you shall say to the Israelites, 'The Lord, the God of your ancestors, the God of Abraham, the God of Isaac, and the God of Jacob, has sent me to you': This is my name forever, and this my title for all generations" (Exodus 3:1-15).

In the Name of the Father, Son, and Holy Spirit.

During the season of Lent the appointed scripture passages continuously demonstrate how God helps people in the wilderness, whatever that wilderness in your life may be. Two weeks ago the appointed scripture passages were about how God helps those in the wilderness of temptation. Today the appointed scriptures are about how God helps those who are stuck in the wilderness.

The collect we prayed today contains a line that cuts against the grain of any form of self-help: "we have no power in ourselves to help ourselves" (*BCP* 218). "We have no power in ourselves to help ourselves"…some of you may completely disagree with this and may find this sermon completely irrelevant…but some of you may have experienced the truth of this.

Americans spend an estimated ten billion dollars a year on self-help products, including a myriad of self-help books. Listen to what was written about self-help books in a recent online article of the acclaimed business magazine *Forbes*:

> The genre is so wide-ranging that Amazon breaks self-help down into 28 subcategories, among them

anger management, creativity, emotions, happiness, inner child, sex, spiritual and success. While of course, many are released at other times of the year, December and January are particularly popular times for many publishers to put out these motivational titles (Rachel Kramer Bussel, January 10, 2019).

Obviously the high sales of self-help books in December and January are due to people making New Year's resolutions. And yet roughly half of these self-help books are never read past the first chapter, and nearly 90% of them are never finished, let alone applied. During Lent many Christians attempt various feats of self-help under the guise of "Lenten disciplines" only to become discouraged and realize that maybe there is some truth to what we prayed in the collect today.

When I was growing up I remember being taught, "The Lord helps those who help themselves." Perhaps you were taught this too. I tried to live by that for many years, only to learn eventually that it is not only untrue but also unbiblical—this idea is found nowhere in scripture. What we read in scripture over and over again are various examples of the exact opposite, the truth that "we have no power in ourselves to help ourselves." But the good news is that we also find the gospel in scripture, a gospel that is a word of comfort and relief for those who need help: "The Lord helps those who *cannot* help themselves." That is the gospel.

Please do not mishear me. Of course working hard, being financially responsible, eating right, developing healthy personal and relational habits are all good things, but when it comes to your salvation—and perhaps other areas in your life—at some point or another you will experience the truth that "The Lord helps those who help themselves" is actually a fallacy, while "The Lords helps those who cannot help themselves" is actually the gospel. If you have not yet experienced this, in the words of one of my favorite Led Zeppelin songs, "You're Time is Gonna Come."

Grace to Help in Time of Need

To be honest and vulnerable with you, I did not really understand this until I experienced it personally and professionally in my mid-thirties. I will spare you the details, but I finally learned the hard way that "The Lord helps those who help themselves" will eventually fall short and you will need the gospel of "The Lord helps those who cannot help themselves." During that season in my life a specific song by another British rock band, Coldplay, spoke right to my heart. The song was written by the lead singer of Coldplay, Chris Martin, for his then-wife Gwyneth Paltrow after her father died. It is a song about help for those who cannot help themselves:

> When you try your best but you don't succeed
> When you get what you want but not what you
>   need
> When you feel so tired but you can't sleep
> Stuck in reverse
> When the tears come streaming down your face
> 'Cause you lose something you can't replace
> When you love someone but it goes to waste
> What could be worse?

And here is the gospel…

> Lights will guide you home
> And ignite your bones
> And I will try to fix you
>
> Tears come streaming down your face
> When you lose something you cannot replace…
> Tears streaming down your face
> I promise I will learn from all my mistakes
>
> Lights will guide you home
> And ignite your bones
> And I will try to fix you
> (From their 2005 album *X & Y*)

Today's passage from the Old Testament book of Exodus is high octane gospel about the Lord helping those who cannot help themselves. Moses, as an adopted son of Pharaoh, had grown up with unimaginable wealth, the best education in the known world, royal privilege upon royal privilege. But as a young man when he saw a fellow Hebrew, who unlike himself was a slave in Egypt, being beaten, he tried to help and ended up killing the instigator and hiding his body, and later fleeing to the wilderness for his life (Exodus 2:11-15). Moses had to leave all his wealth and privilege behind and later began working as a shepherd, a job Egyptians utterly despised, and not even for himself, but for his father-in-law. Scripture tells Moses was not just in the wilderness but that "he led his flock beyond the wilderness, and came to Horeb, the mountain of God" (Exodus 3:1), where one of the most famous episodes in scripture took place:

> There the angel of the Lord appeared to him in a flame of fire out of a bush; he looked, and the bush was blazing, yet it was not consumed. Then Moses said, "I must turn aside and look at this great sight, and see why the bush is not burned up." When the Lord saw that he had turned aside to see, God called to him out of the bush, "Moses, Moses!" And he said, "Here I am." Then he said, "Come no closer! Remove the sandals from your feet, for the place on which you are standing is holy ground." He said further, "I am the God of your father, the God of Abraham, the God of Isaac, and the God of Jacob." And Moses hid his face, for he was afraid to look at God (Exodus 3:2-6).

Moses had earlier learned the hard way that in spite of his wealth and education and royal privilege, when it came to helping himself, it all fell short, and so Moses ended up being the perfect person for God to call to help his fellow Israelites who had been enslaved in Egypt for four centuries, fellow Israelites who likewise could not help themselves—as the writer of Exodus continues:

> Then the Lord said, "I have observed the misery of my people who are in Egypt; I have heard their cry on account of their taskmasters. Indeed I know their sufferings, and I have come down to deliver them from the Egyptians, and to bring them up out of that land to a good and broad land, a land flowing with milk and honey...So come, I will send you to Pharaoh to bring my people, the Israelites, out of Egypt" (Exodus 3:7-10).

Does Moses jump at this opportunity because he thinks he is a hero who will save the day for his fellow Israelites? Hardly, as he asked, "Who am I that I should go to Pharaoh, and bring out the Israelites out of Egypt?" In response, God assured him, "I will be with you." But Moses continued, "If I come to the Israelites and say to them, 'The God of your ancestors has sent me to you,' and they ask me, 'What is his name?' what shall I say to them?" And as you probably know, God replied, "I Am Who I Am...Thus you shall say to the Israelites, 'I Am has sent me to you... The Lord, the God of your ancestors, the God of Abraham, the God of Isaac, and the God of Jacob, has sent me to you'" (Exodus 3:11-15).

God did exactly what he told Moses he would do; he sent Moses, was with Moses, and through Moses delivered the Israelites from four centuries of slavery in Egypt, and went on to sustain them through forty years in the wilderness, and eventually brought them to the "good and broad land, a land flowing with milk and honey." In other words, the Lord helped those who could not help themselves. The heart of Moses' ministry was his dependence on God's help, for scripture describes him as "very humble, more so than anyone else on the face of the earth" (Numbers 12:3).

This episode from the Old Testament foreshadowed what happened many centuries later when another shepherd in the wilderness, Jesus, the Good Shepherd, would save not just the Israelites but the whole world. With humility that surpassed even Moses,

Jesus willingly left heaven and became incarnate not only as a human being, but as a slave, in order to save a world enslaved to sin and death, in order to help a world full of people unable to help themselves, including you.

The same One who met Moses when he was stuck in the wilderness and not only changed the whole direction of his life but of the entire nation of Israel has observed the misery in your life, has heard your cries for help, and has known all your sufferings. And out of unconditional love for you Jesus journeyed beyond the wilderness to a different mountain of God, Calvary, where he died in order to help a world unable to help itself.

The same One who called Moses repeatedly by name, calls you by name (John 10:3). The same One who assured Moses, "I will be with you," is with you: "Emmanuel…God with us" (Matthew 1:23). The same One revealed his identity as I Am Who I Am over and over: "I Am the Bread of Life who will feed you in the wilderness…I Am the Good Shepherd who calls you by name…I Am the Door that is open to you when every other door you have tried have been locked shut…I Am the Way when you are lost, I Am the Truth when you have been lied to again and again, I Am the Life when you feel dead inside…I Am the Resurrection and the Life who assures you that death is not the end of the story" (John 6:35; 10:11; 10:7; 14:6; and 11:25).

Think about your life for a moment. Is there an area where you are stuck in the wilderness, an area that defies every self-help book you have ever started reading, where you try your best and you don't succeed, where you get what you want but not what you need, where you feel so tired but you can't sleep, where you are stuck in reverse? The Lord helps you "when the tears come streaming down your face." The Lord helps you when "you lose something you can't replace." The Lord helps you "when you love someone but it goes to waste." The Lord helps you when it cannot get any worse. The Lord's office is at rock bottom, at the end of your rope.

And Jesus Christ, the Light of the World (John 8:12) "will guide you home and ignite your bones" and will not just "try to fix you" but will actually save you.

The gospel is good news for those stuck in the wilderness, good news for those who have learned the hard way that they have no power in themselves to help themselves because the gospel is that the Lord helps those who cannot help themselves.

Amen.

Totally Unbelievable and Yet Completely True

Then Jesus said, "There was a man who had two sons. The younger of them said to his father, 'Father, give me the share of the property that will belong to me.' So he divided his property between them. A few days later the younger son gathered all he had and traveled to a distant country, and there he squandered his property in dissolute living. When he had spent everything, a severe famine took place throughout that country, and he began to be in need. So he went and hired himself out to one of the citizens of that country, who sent him to his fields to feed the pigs. He would gladly have filled himself with the pods that the pigs were eating; and no one gave him anything. But when he came to himself he said, 'How many of my father's hired hands have bread enough and to spare, but here I am dying of hunger! I will get up and go to my father, and I will say to him, "Father, I have sinned against heaven and before you; I am no longer worthy to be called your son; treat me like one of your hired hands."' So he set off and went to his father. But while he was still far off, his father saw him and was filled with compassion; he ran and put his arms around him and kissed him. Then the son said to him, 'Father, I have sinned against heaven and before you; I am no longer worthy to be called your son.' But the father said to his slaves, 'Quickly, bring out a robe—the best one—and put it on him; put a ring on his finger and sandals on his feet. And get the fatted calf and kill it, and let us eat and celebrate; for this son of mine was dead and is alive again; he was lost and is found!' And they began to celebrate" (Luke 15:11-24).

In the Name of the Father, Son, and Holy Spirit.

Major League Baseball had its Opening Day last week, one of my favorite reminders that spring has officially arrived. On October 18, 1977 something totally unbelievable and yet completely true happened during game six of the World Series. I was in third grade and remember watching as New York Yankees slugger Reggie Jackson hit not one, not two, but three home runs off only three pitches, each pitch from a different pitcher.

In the fourth inning, he stepped to the plate and Los Angeles Dodgers pitcher Burt Hooten threw a low ball that Jackson ripped into the right field seats. In the fifth inning, Dodger relief pitcher Elias Sosa's first pitch to Jackson was likewise drilled into the right field bleachers. And then, in the eighth inning, with all of Yankee Stadium on their feet chanting, "Reggie! Reggie! Reggie!" Jackson walks to the plate, and then crushes Charlie Hough's knuckleball about 475 feet into the center field bleachers, and Yankee Stadium erupts. Three consecutive pitches, each from a different pitcher, three consecutive homeruns, in one World Series game. I got chills watching that night. It was totally unbelievable and yet completely true.

Today's gospel reading, the Parable of the Prodigal Son, is the most gospel-loaded, gospel-replete, gospel-inundated, gospel-waterlogged, gospel-full of all of Jesus' parables. If you ever want to know what God is like, what the grace of God is like, what forgiveness from God is like, if you ever want to know the heart of what the gospel is all about, what the love of God is like, look no further than the Parable of the Prodigal Son. This parable is the biblical motherlode of God's grace.

The context of this parable is very important. Luke tells us, "Now all the tax collectors and sinners were coming near to listen to [Jesus]. And the Pharisees and the scribes were grumbling and saying, 'This fellow welcomes sinners and eats with them'" (Luke 15:1-2). Jesus was not only friendly to and friendly with "tax collectors and sinners," both of whom were utterly despised by the religious leaders, the Pharisees and scribes, Jesus also welcomed them and ate with them.

Jesus did not just tolerate tax collectors and sinners, he liked them, and they could tell he was not faking it, which is why they enjoyed hanging out with him. All of this completely undid the Pharisees and scribes. They could not understand how Jesus could hang out with "those people." And so they did what many people often do when faced with something they do not understand, they grumbled.

And Jesus responded to the grumbling of the scribes and Pharisees by telling them three parables in a row. In the fourth inning of this dinner party Jesus walked up to plate and hit his first home run, the Parable of the Lost Sheep. Jesus talked about how God loves you not only corporately but individually, so much so that if you were one of a hundred sheep and you were the only one lost, God would leave the other ninety-nine sheep and search for you until he found you. Then he would lay you gently on his shoulders, carry you home, and then throw a party for all his neighbors because he we so happy that he found the one lost sheep, you—"Rejoice with me, for I have found my sheep that was lost" (Luke 15:6).

Then again in the fifth inning of this dinner party Jesus stepped to the plate, and hit his second homerun, the Parable of the Lost Coin. Jesus described God's love for you being like a lady who has ten silver coins, but loses one of them. She then sweeps the house, looks under every piece of furniture, looks in every drawer, under every carpet, in every nook and cranny of her house until she finds the one lost coin. Then just like the shepherd, she calls her friends together to celebrate because she is so happy that she found the one lost coin, you—"Rejoice with me, for I have found the coin that I had lost" (Luke 15:9).

Then in the eighth inning of this same dinner party, with all the sinners and tax collectors on the edge of their seats wondering what parable Jesus would say next, Jesus walked again to the plate and launched his third homerun deep into centerfield, the Parable of the Prodigal Son. This parable, just like the first two, demonstrates what God's love for you is really like. It is a love so great that it does not make sense. Wouldn't a shepherd who still had ninety-nine out of the hundred sheep cut his losses and move on? Apparently not. God's love for you is much greater than that. Wouldn't a lady who still had her nine other silver coins be satisfied with that and forget about the one that was lost? Again, apparently not, because, again, God's love for you is much greater than that. God's love for you is totally unbelievable and yet completely true.

In the Parable of the Prodigal Son, Jesus described how a very wealthy man had two sons, the dutiful firstborn, and his slacker younger brother. The younger brother was not only a slacker, he was utterly rude and disrespectful to his father, and demanded, "Father, give me the share of the property that will belong to me." In other words, he wished his father were dead so he could have his inheritance now. The father did not argue with his younger son or put him in his place; instead, as Luke tells us, "He divided his property between them."

Shortly thereafter the younger son takes off and goes "to a distant country and, there he squandered his property in dissolute living." It is not unlike what many people do when they go to Las Vegas or on a "girls' trip." But after he had maxed out every credit card, cleaned out every bank account with his ATM card, liquidated every IRA account, spent every dollar and cent in his pockets, Jesus said, "a severe famine took place throughout that country, and he began to be in need" (Luke 15:11-14). The rich kid who had never wanted for anything ever in his life now had nothing—and it was his fault, and he knew it.

He was so desperate he became a servant whose job it was to slop the pigs, and remember—Jews were forbidden to eat pork because it was deemed unclean. Moreover, he became so hungry that he wished he could eat the same slop he was feeding the pigs—and no one cared, no one would help, or as Luke writes, "no one gave him anything." And it was in that moment—broke, filthy, alone, starving, friendless—that the younger brother decided maybe it was time to go back home.

The problem was that he had been a total jerk to his father, had wasted in a very short time "on dissolute living" what it had taken his father a very long time to earn, and had tarnished his family name. He was convinced that if he indeed went home, things would never be the same again, so he prepared a speech for his father, "Father, I have sinned against heaven and before you; I am no longer worthy to be called your son" (Luke 15:15-19). And as he rehearsed this speech again and again, the younger brother stumbled toward home.

What Jesus then described is that the love of God is totally unbelievable and yet completely true, that the grace of God is greater than the law. In his 2007 book *Grace in Practice* Paul Zahl describes how in the long run a child will respond much more to grace from their parents than they will to the law:

> You can learn about this absolute separation between grace and law if you listen to your children. Children never respond well to a lecture. Is there a case on record of children responding well to a lecture? They may assent by a reluctant nod or a sort of grudging silence. But it is all resistance. When you are dying, it

will come back to you. Your children will tell you the incidents that made a difference to them. They will tell you the moments when they heard the true voice of parental love. Believe me, it was rare. It was rarer than you ever thought. It took place in connection with your daughter's divorce and the way you didn't say a word of "I told you so" when she walked in the door with her six-year-old daughter and no more husband (85-86).

Then Paul Zahl recounts this true story:

> Or maybe the grace came out after your son's car crash. Rod Rosenbladt, a Lutheran theologian, tells the true story of wrecking his father's Buick 8 when he was sixteen years old. Rod was drunk, as were all his friends who were in the car. The first thing Rod's dad asked him over the phone was whether he was all right. Rod said yes. He also told his father he was drunk. Later that night, Rod wept and wept in his father's study. At the end of the ordeal, his father said one thing: "How about tomorrow we go get you a new car." Rod says now that he became a theist in that moment. God's grace became real… Rod's father spoke the word of grace in that moment. In that eternal encounter, for it reflected the mechanism of God's grace, there was no law. The law's dominion came to an end. Grace superseded it (86).

As you can expect, some people bristle at this example of grace. Where was the lesson of responsibility? How was Rod held accountable? Where was the penance? Where was the lecture? Every time Rod has shared that totally unbelievable and yet completely true story about grace from his father he has gotten resistance and pushback. From whom? From people who just like the Pharisees and tax collectors in today's gospel passage grumbled about Jesus' friendship with sinners. In the Parable of the Prodigal Son, Jesus went on to say that when the younger brother was "still far off, his father saw him and was filled with compassion" and "he ran and put his arms around him and kissed him."

The prodigal son was probably stunned that his distinguished, wealthy father not only acknowledged his existence but ran to him (something elderly people at that time would never do) and hugged and kissed his filthy, smelly, broke, self. Then he tells his father the speech that he had rehearsed countless times during his long walk home, "Father, I have sinned against heaven and before you; I am no longer worthy to be called your son" (Luke 15:20-21).

And how did the father respond to his son's speech? Did he say, "You're right, you have sinned against heaven and me. How dare you! How could you have the audacity to ask for your inheritance when I was still alive? How could you wish I were dead? Have I not always given you everything you wanted? You have shamed me, and you have shamed my family. You are not worthy to be called my son and you never will be. Things will never be the same again"? Did the father say all that? No. But wouldn't the father use this opportunity to put his younger son in his place and teach him a lesson? Apparently not.

Instead, just like Rod's father, the father of the prodigal son "spoke the word of grace in that moment" as he paused just long enough from hugging and kissing his son only to order his servants, "Quickly, bring out a robe—the best one—and put it on him; put a ring on his finger and sandals on his feet…let us eat and celebrate for this son of mine was dead and is alive again; he was lost and is found!" (Luke 15:22-24). The best robe was always given to the guest of honor, the ring was the symbol of authority, and sandals were only worn by children. The younger brother was right: when he got home things would indeed never be the same again, but in the exact opposite way he expected because "the law's dominion came to an end," because "grace superseded it." And his father threw a party to end all parties.

Not too long after hitting these three homerun parables, Jesus heard the crowd not just grumbling, "This fellow welcomes sinners and eats with them," but chanting something much darker, "Crucify him! Crucify him!" And Jesus was crucified for all the grumblers and all the prodigals of the world, including you. And on Good Friday, "the law's dominion came to an end" because "grace superseded it."

That is what the gospel is all about, that is what the love of God for you is like…totally unbelievable and yet completely true.

Amen.

Defined by the Grace of God

If anyone else has reason to be confident in the flesh, I have more: circumcised on the eighth day, a member of the people of Israel, of the tribe of Benjamin, a Hebrew born of Hebrews; as to the law, a Pharisee; as to zeal, a persecutor of the church; as to righteousness under the law, blameless. Yet whatever gains I had, these I have come to regard as loss because of Christ. More than that, I regard everything as loss because of the surpassing value of knowing Christ Jesus my Lord. For his sake I have suffered the loss of all things, and I regard them as rubbish, in order that I may gain Christ as be found in him, not having a righteousness of my own that comes from the law, but one that comes through faith in Christ, the righteousness from God based on faith. I want to know Christ and the power of his resurrection and the sharing of his sufferings by becoming like him in his death, if somehow I may attain the resurrection from the dead. Not that I have already obtained this or have already reached the goal; but I press on to make it my own, because Christ Jesus has made me his own. Beloved, I do not consider that I have made it my own; but this one thing I do: forgetting what lies behind and straining forward to what lies ahead, I press on toward the goal for the prize of the heavenly call of God in Christ (Philippians 3:4-14).

In the Name of the Father, Son, and Holy Spirit.

Lent is a season of repentance during which we are reminded of our mortality as on Ash Wednesday ashes are imposed on our foreheads with the words, "Remember that you are dust and to dust you shall return" (*BCP* 265). So with that in mind, let me ask you a rather morbid question—if you were to write your own obituary, what would you write? What defines who you are and what your life is all about?

Many people define themselves based on what has or has not been done *by* them—their professional accomplishments, or their academic achievement, or their athletic prowess or musical talent or creative ability or lack of any of the above. Some people define themselves based on their family—how wealthy or distinguished or revered their family is in the community, or by how successful or unsuccessful their kids may be. Some people define themselves by the college they attended (or their kids attend) or what college they root for, or by their political party or their sexuality, or their relationship status, or by what kind of vehicle they drive, or where they go for vacation, or what part of the country they are from, or what kind of music they like. Some people define themselves by the bad things or wrong things they have done.

Other people do not define themselves by what has been done *by* them, but by what has been done *to* them—by a physical illness, or by a tragedy like an untimely death in the family, or by being the victim of abuse, or by being done wrong by some corporation or the government or the school system or the church. They are victims who are defined by what has been done to them.

Sometimes Christians define themselves as Evangelical or Catholic or Pentecostal, or by what denomination they belong to—Baptist or Southern Baptist or Presbyterian or Methodist or Assemblies of God or "non-denom." There are approximately thirty-five major Christian denominations in the United States and hundreds more minor denominations. In fact, it's very American that if you have had enough of your current denomination, you can even start a new one.

Or how about clergy in the Episcopal Church? Did you go to Virginia Theological Seminary, or Sewanee, or Berkeley Divinity School at Yale, or Nashotah House or some (God forbid) non-Episcopal seminary? Are you liturgically "high church" or "low church" or "broad church"? Do you wear a chasuble or a cassock alb or a cassock and surplice? Do you use only the 1979 *Book of Common Prayer*, or do you use new experimental liturgies, or do you insist on only using the 1928 *Book of Common Prayer*? Do you wear a Roman style collar or an Anglican style collar? Is the music at your church strictly traditional hymnody or renewal or contemporary? Do you prefer to be called "Father so-and-so" or "Mother so-and-so" or not? You may think I am being silly, but Episcopal clergy are quite susceptible to defining themselves in these ways.

But when it comes to the gospel, we are ultimately defined neither by what has been done *by* us nor by what has been done *to* us. Instead, we are defined by what has been done *for* us—and not just for us but for the whole world—in the death and resurrection of Jesus Christ. The defining word about your life belongs neither to you nor to anyone else, but to God. You are defined by the grace of God.

During his second missionary journey the Apostle Paul planted the first Christian church in Europe, the church in Philippi. The first members of this church included a wealthy merchant named Lydia who led a women's prayer group that met by the river, a slave-girl out of whom Paul had cast a demon, and a jailer and his family. The planting of this church in Philippi involved what you may expect, preaching of the gospel of God's unconditional love and grace in Jesus Christ—which is the only true gospel—and a prayer group, but also what you may not expect, including Paul conducting an exorcism, being arrested and flogged by Roman soldiers, being imprisoned and chained to a wall only to experience an earthquake during which his chains fell off and he was free to go. But instead of fleeing the prison, Paul remained and baptized the jailor and his family (Acts 16).

Most books, seminars or workshops about church planting include marketing strategies and demographic research and action plans, not exorcisms, imprisonment and earthquakes. But the Holy Spirit moved through the Apostle Paul and the Holy Spirit moved through those events and created the first church in Europe. Several years later the Apostle Paul was imprisoned again, this time in Rome, and while there he wrote his Letter to the Philippians.

In today's passage from the third chapter of this letter Paul describes how he was not defined by what had been done by him even though his religious pedigree and background are quite impressive:

> If anyone else has reason to be confident in the flesh, I have more: circumcised on the eighth day, a member of the people of Israel, of the tribe of Benjamin, a Hebrew born of Hebrews; as to the law, a Pharisee; as to zeal, a persecutor of the church; as to righteousness under the law, blameless (Philippians 3:4-6).

If you unpack this you will find that Paul's being circumcised on the eighth day was in accordance with Old Testament law (Leviticus 12:3), that Paul was a pureblooded Hebrew—as opposed to being of mixed ethnic descent like the despised Samaritans, that he was from the tribe of Benjamin—one of the two sons of Jacob's favorite wife Rachel, that he was a brilliant Pharisee whose passion for keeping God's law was so strong he persecuted the church whose faith was not founded on keeping God's law but on God's forgiveness and love in Jesus Christ.

And yet Paul would not define himself by any of those positive things done by him. Neither would Paul define himself by the negative things done by him, as he wrote to his protégé Timothy: "I was formerly a blasphemer, a persecutor, and a man of violence"

(1 Timothy 1:13). Nor would Paul define himself by what had been done to him, even his sufferings for the sake of the gospel, which he delineates in his Second Letter to the Corinthians:

> Five times I have received the forty lashes minus one. Three times I was beaten with rods. Once I received a stoning. Three times I was shipwrecked; for a night and a day I was adrift at sea…in toil and hardship, through many a sleepless night, hungry and thirsty, often without food, cold and naked. And besides other things, I am under daily pressure because of my anxiety for all the churches (2 Corinthians 11:24-25, 27- 28).

Paul knew that he was neither defined by what had been done by him nor by what had been done to him, but by what had been done for him. Paul knew that he was defined by the grace of God, a grace he personally experienced in an encounter with the Risen Jesus on the road to Damascus (Acts 9:1-9), a grace that marked a brand new direction for his life.

To Timothy, Paul wrote, "The grace of our Lord overflowed for me with the faith and love that are in Christ Jesus. The saying is sure and worthy of full acceptance, that Christ Jesus came in the world to save sinners—of whom I am the foremost" (1 Timothy 1:14-15). To the Corinthians, Paul wrote again about the grace of God, "[God] said to me, 'My grace is sufficient for you, for power is made perfect in weakness.' So I will boast all the more gladly of my weaknesses, so that the power of Christ may dwell in me" (2 Corinthians 12:9). And again in today's passage from his Letter to the Philippians, after setting forth his impressive religious pedigree and background Paul continues:

> Yet whatever gains I had, these I have come to regard as loss because of Christ. More than that, I regard everything as loss because of the surpassing value of knowing Christ Jesus my Lord. For his sake I have

suffered the loss of all things, and I regard them as rubbish, in order that I may gain Christ as be found in him, not having a righteousness of my own that comes from the law, but one that comes through faith in Christ, the righteousness from God based on faith. I want to know Christ and the power of his resurrection and the sharing of his sufferings by becoming like him in his death, if somehow I may attain the resurrection from the dead (Philippians 3:7-11).

Paul refused to define himself by what was done *by* him or *to* him, but instead defined himself by what God had done *for* him, "I regard everything as loss because of the surpassing value of knowing Christ Jesus my Lord…I regard them as rubbish, in order that I may gain Christ and be found in him." What is true for Paul is true for you. Ultimately, you are not defined by what has been done by you or to you but rather what God has done for you. Through faith, trust, in Jesus Christ you have received righteousness, or right standing, with God. Paul then describes how this grace of God gives us the ability to press on:

> Not that I have already obtained this or have already reached the goal; but I press on to make it my own, because Christ Jesus has made me his own. Beloved, I do not consider that I have made it my own; but this one thing I do: forgetting what lies behind and straining forward to what lies ahead, I press on toward the goal for the prize of the heavenly call of God in Christ (Philippians 3:12-14).

The grace of God not only defined Paul's life, it gave him a brand new start in his life—"I press on to make it my own, because Christ Jesus has made me his own…forgetting what lies behind and straining forward to what lies ahead, I press on." Paul did not define his life by what had been done by him or to him, but for him by the grace of God. In this Letter to the Galatians he put it this way: "The life I now live in the flesh I live by faith in the Son of

God, who loved me and gave himself for me" (Galatians 2:20). The grace of God defined who Paul was and what his life was all about.

Think about your life for a moment. Perhaps you have defined your life by the good things done by you, or things that should have been done by you but you dropped the ball or did not follow through. Or maybe you have defined your life by the wrong things done by you, things that if you could go back and undo you would, but there is no rewind button for your life. Or perhaps you have had some awful things done to you or said to you that have defined your life or how you see your life.

The gospel transcends all that. Your life is defined by the grace of God.

The grace of God gives you a brand new start. The grace of God gives you the ability to press on—to press on regardless of what has been done by you, to press on regardless of what has been done to you, to press on because of what God has done for you, to press on because Jesus Christ loved you and gave himself for you and made you his own. The grace of God reminds you that you are a beloved child of the loving God.

The grace of God means that you are indeed what will be said at the commendation prayer at your funeral: a sheep of God's own fold, a lamb of God's own flock, a sinner of God's own redeeming (*BCP* 483).

So regardless of what you would write in your own obituary, regardless of what others would write in your obituary, God's obituary for you has already been written by the blood of Jesus Christ shed on the cross, and it reads, "Fully known, fully forgiven, fully loved."

You are defined by the grace of God.
Amen.

The Faithful Love of Your Humble God

A Palm Sunday Sermon

> *Let the same mind be in you that was in Christ Jesus who, though he was in the form of God, did not regard equality with God as something to be exploited, but emptied himself, taking the form of a slave, being born in human likeness. And being found in human form, he humbled himself and became obedient to the point of death—even death on a cross. Therefore God also highly exalted him and gave him the name that is above every name, so that at the name of Jesus every knee should bend, in heaven and on earth and under the earth, and every tongue should confess that Jesus Christ is Lord, to the glory of God the Father (Philippians 2:5-11).*

In the Name of the Father, Son, and Holy Spirit.

Since my family and I lived in Charlottesville, Virginia, for eleven years before moving to Valdosta, there is no way I can avoid talking about the University of Virginia's first ever men's basketball national championship last week. But first, a little background from last year…

On March 16, 2018, the UVA Men's basketball team became the first number one seed to ever lose to a sixteen seed in the first round of the March Madness tournament. Prior to that game sixteen seed teams were a combined 0–135 against one seeds. Going into that game against number the sixteen seed University of Maryland, Baltimore County Retrievers the Virginia Cavaliers were twenty point favorites. They had a record of 31–3, had set the record for most ACC wins in a season and had just won the ACC tournament. But instead of winning by twenty points, as had been predicted, number one seeded UVA lost to the sixteen seed by twenty points, 74-54. At the postgame press conference UVA coach Tony Bennett put it this way:

> We got whipped. It wasn't even close… I told our guys we had a historic season, a historic season in terms of most wins in the ACC. A week ago we were cutting down the nets and the confetti was falling. And then we make history by being the first one-seed to lose. I'm sure a lot of people will be happy about that, and it stings.

Coach Bennett later revealed in an interview with *USA Today* that as humiliating as that loss had been, there had still been an upside:

> I'm thankful for what happened because it drew me closer to my faith in the Lord, drew me closer to my wife and children, just because you realize what's unconditional. In those spots when the world is telling you you're a failure, you're a loser, and you're the worst thing going and all that stuff you say, "OK, what really matters?"

In their first round game of this year's March Madness tournament, UVA, again a number one seed, found themselves again trailing to the sixteen seed Gardener-Webb University Runnin' Bulldogs by fourteen points in the first half. Everyone was thinking, "Here we go again," but they rallied and won. And last Monday night they won the national championship in overtime 85–77 over Texas Tech. When the final whistle blew and UVA had capped their historic worst to first run, Coach Bennett bowed his head and simply said, "Thank you. I'm humbled, Lord." And when he talked to his team in the locker room afterward, he told them, "Promise me you'll remain humble. Don't let this change you."

No doubt last week Tony Bennett and the players who had experienced that "worst to first" run with him received lots of cheers and kudos from the very same people who had told them last year, "You're a failure, you're a loser, and you're the worst thing going." People can be so fickle.

Along these lines in 1923, Jimmy Cox wrote a song that became a blues standard, a song entitled "Nobody Knows You When You're Down and Out." It has been performed by many artists but most famously by Eric Clapton and his fellow bandmates of Derek and the Dominos on their masterpiece 1970 double album *Layla and Other Assorted Love Songs* as Clapton sings:

> Once I lived the life of a millionaire
> Spent all my money, I just did not care
> Took all my friends out for a good time
> Bought bootleg liquor, champagne and wine
> Then I began to fall so low
> Lost all my good friends
> I did not have nowhere to go…
>
> 'Cause nobody knows you
> When you're down and out
> In your pocket not one penny
> And as for friends you don't have any
>
> When you finally get back up on your feet again
> Everybody wants to be your long-lost friend
> It's mighty strange without a doubt
> Nobody knows you when you're down and out

On this Palm Sunday, we are reminded that during the final week of Jesus' earthly life he went from first to worst. At his triumphal entry people were metaphorically "cutting down the nets" and "the confetti was falling," or rather the palm branches were falling, onto the road upon which Jesus entered Jerusalem, with shouts of "Blessed is he that comes in the Name of the Lord! Hosanna in the highest!" chanted by the crowd. Later that same week the crowd began chanting something quite different: "Crucify him! Crucify him!" And the crowd got what they wanted, and Jesus was crucified. In five days, Jesus went from first to worst in the most horrifying and painful way imaginable.

The crowds during Holy Week could not have been any more fickle, and yet Jesus could not have remained any more faithful. And Jesus also remained humble. None of the fickleness of the crowds changed him, not at all. Palm Sunday is always a stark reminder of the fickleness of people and the faithfulness of God.

In his Letter to the Philippians the Apostle Paul emphasizes the importance of humility in the church. In the verses immediately preceding today's passage he wrote, "Do nothing from selfish ambition or conceit, but in humility regard others as better than yourselves. Let each of you look not to your own interests, but to the interests of others" (Philippians 2:3-4).

Then the apostle points to the ultimate example of what this looks like by describing the humility of our Lord and Savior Jesus Christ:

> Let the same mind be in you that was in Christ Jesus, who, though he was in the form of God, did not regard equality with God as something to be exploited, but emptied himself, taking the form of a slave, being born in human likeness. And being found in human form, he humbled himself and became obedient to the point of death—even death on a cross (Philippians 2:5-8).

Jesus humbled himself in becoming a human being at his incarnation, and humbled himself again in becoming a servant. In response to his disciples arguing among themselves who was the greatest, Jesus had told them this about his humility, "The Son of Man came not to be served but to serve, and to give his life a ransom for many" (Mark 10:45). Jesus had also taught, "All who exalt themselves will be humbled, and all who humble themselves will be exalted" (Matthew 23:12).

Jesus did not just teach about this kind of humility, he lived it. He humbled himself yet again at the Last Supper and washed the disciples' feet—including, yes, even Judas Iscariot's feet—and the next day humbled himself yet again in dying on a cross, a death so ignominious, so degrading, so awful, so humiliating that Roman citizens were not lawfully allowed to be crucified. But Jesus was not a Roman citizen. Jesus was the Humble King of a kingdom marked by humility and love, the Kingdom of God.

As Jesus the Humble King suffered that humiliating death on the cross, passersby derided him, "You're a failure, you're a loser, and you're the worst thing going." And Jesus just took it. And Jesus just kept humbling himself. And Jesus just kept praying, "Father, forgive them; they do not know what they are doing" (Luke 23:34). And then Jesus just died. His humiliating suffering and death were over. On a cosmic scale and for the sake of a fickle world, Jesus had humbled himself to the ultimate degree and gone from first to worst. Jesus did nothing from selfish ambition. He considered others, including you, better than himself. And how did God the Father respond to this humility of his Son? Paul continues:

> Therefore God also highly exalted him and gave him the name that is above every name, so that at the name of Jesus every knee should bend, in heaven and on earth and under the earth, and every tongue should confess that Jesus Christ is Lord, to the glory of God the Father (Philippians 2:9-11).

Jesus was raised from the lowest place, the grave, and exalted to the highest place, the right hand of the Father. You could say Jesus' humility took him from first to worst and back to first again. And the

Risen Jesus remains as humble and faithful as ever, bearing on his hands and feet and side for all eternity the scars of his humiliating death for a fickle world, the scars of his humiliating death for you.

So on this Palm Sunday, may the Holy Spirit help you "realize what's unconditional" and remind you "what really matters": the faithful love of your humble God, who not only knows you when you're down and out, but also loves you when you're down and out. Finally, scripture tells us the only proper way to respond to the faithful love of your humble God, "Humble yourselves in the sight of the Lord, and he shall lift you up" (James 4:10, KJV).

Amen.

Jesus was Rejected for You

A Good Friday Sermon

He was despised and rejected by others; a man of suffering and acquainted with infirmity; and as one from whom others hide their faces he was despised, and we held him of no account (Isaiah 53:3).

In the Name of the Father, Son, and Holy Spirit.

Every year on Good Friday we read a passage from the great Old Testament prophet Isaiah, whose ministry among the Israelites took place about seven centuries before Christ, a prophetic passage about the passion and death of Jesus Christ, the Messiah, the Son of God. This passage is saturated with details about Jesus' substitutionary suffering and death in your place, as Isaiah wrote:

> Surely he has borne our infirmities and carried our diseases; yet we accounted him stricken, struck down by God, and afflicted. But he was wounded for our transgressions, crushed for our iniquities; upon him was the punishment that made us whole, and by his bruises we are healed. All we like sheep have gone astray; we have all turned to our own way, and the Lord has laid on him the iniquity of us all (Isaiah 53:4-6).

On Good Friday, Jesus suffered in your place and died in your place. Today I am preaching briefly on something else Jesus did on Good Friday: he was rejected in your place—as Isaiah also wrote: "He was despised and rejected by others; a man of suffering and acquainted with infirmity; and as one from whom others hide their faces he was despised, and we held him of no account" (Isaiah 53:3).

Jesus was rejected for you, which means you are accepted by God.

The fear of rejection is one of the most common fears human beings have. In an online article for *Psychology Today*, Dr. John Amodeo put it this way:

> The fear of rejection is one of our deepest human fears. Biologically wired with a longing to belong, we fear being seen in a critical way. We're anxious about the prospect of being cut off, demeaned or isolated… we may be afraid that rejection confirms our worst fear—perhaps that we're unlovable, or that we're destined to be alone, or that we have little worth or value. When these fear-based thoughts keep spinning in our mind, we may become agitated, anxious, or depressed (April 4, 2014).

Some people are rejected as children, and such rejection can leave lifelong scars. John Steinbeck described this in his classic 1952 novel *East of Eden*:

> The greatest terror a child can have is that he is not loved, and rejection is the hell he fears. I think everyone in the world to a large or small extent has felt rejection. And with rejection comes anger, and with anger some kind of crime in revenge for the rejection, and with the crime guilt—and there is the story of mankind (Penguin Classics edition 270).

The greatest king in the history of Israel, David, was rejected by his family. Scripture tells us when the prophet Samuel came to visit David's family in Bethlehem in order to anoint one of the sons of his father Jesse as the next king of Israel, David was not even invited. Jesse presented all seven of David's older brothers to Samuel only to have Samuel respond each time, "Neither has the Lord chosen this one." Earlier the Lord had told Samuel, "The Lord does not see as mortals see; they look on the outward appearance, but the Lord looks on the heart."

After seeing all seven of David's older brothers, the prophet Samuel asked Jesse, "Are all your sons here?" to which Jesse responded, "There remains yet the youngest, but he is keeping the sheep." Jesse would not even refer to David, his rejected youngest son, by his name. And yet Samuel replied, "Send and bring him; for we will not sit down until he comes here." So Jesse and his seven older sons and Samuel all stood waiting for the arrival of the rejected son, the rejected shepherd, David. When David finally arrived, the Lord told Samuel, "Rise and anoint him; for this is the one"—and scripture continues, "Then Samuel took the horn of oil, and anointed him in the presence of his brothers; and the spirit of the Lord came mightily upon David from that day forward" (1 Samuel 16:1-13).

And although David had been, and would continue to be, rejected by his family, he had been, and would continue to be, accepted by the Lord—accepted by the Lord who knew his broken heart, accepted by the Lord who had always been with him as he shepherded sheep in the wilderness during those long days and longer nights, accepted by the Lord who had called him and anointed him to be the next king of Israel, accepted by the Lord who would never ever reject him. And David knew this, which is why he later wrote in Psalm 27, "Though my father and my mother forsake me, the Lord will sustain me" (Psalm 27:14, *BCP* 618).

In the gospel-soaked 2017 film *Wonder,* Jacob Tremblay plays

Auggie Pullman, a boy who was born with Treacher Collins syndrome, which means his facial bones did not form properly, leaving his face extremely disfigured, even after multiple reconstructive surgeries. At the beginning of the film Auggie refuses to go out in public without wearing his astronaut helmet, not just because he dreamed of going to the stars, but because he was embarrassed by his disfigured face and the ridicule it inevitably drew.

But although Auggie was no longer allowed to wear his astronaut helmet, he persevered through an entire difficult school year. As his father Nate, played by Owen Wilson, helps him get ready for the end of the school year assembly, there is a beautiful moment of grace. Nate is tying Auggie's tie and says, "You've come a long way, huh?" "Yeah," Auggie replies. "I am proud of you for sticking it out," Nate continues. Auggie grins, "You didn't think I would, did you?" Nate lies, "Of course I did," but after seeing Auggie's dubious expression continues, "Okay, well, come on, when you started you were still wearing the astronaut helmet in public." "I love that helmet," Auggie says, "I wish I knew where it was."

Nate pauses and looks Auggie in the eye. "It's in my office." Auggie is very upset. "What?!" "Auggie," Nate pleas, "please don't be mad. You gotta understand—you were wearing it all the time. I never got to see you anymore. I missed your face. I know you don't always like it, but I love it. It's my son's face. I wanna see it. Do you forgive me?" Auggie says, "No...yes," and then asks, "Does mom know?" "No, God no," Nate replies, "She'd kill me, but I can maybe find it if you need it back." But Auggie shakes his head: "That's okay," and Nate hugs Auggie and gazes proudly into his beloved son's face. Although Auggie was often rejected by the world, he was never rejected by his family.

But some people have been rejected by their family in one way or another—rejected by parents, or siblings, or a spouse (or ex-spouse), or even their children—or rejected in other areas like school, or work, or yes, even church. Such experiences of rejection are often then placed on their relationship with God. In other words, because they have been rejected by others, they feel rejected by God—rejected by God because they have made big mistakes in their life, rejected by God because they have been rejected by the church, rejected and alone in the wilderness with the sheep, rejected and therefore uninvited.

In his passion and death Jesus was rejected—rejected by the world he had created, rejected by his fellow Israelites as scripture tells us, "He came to what was his own, and his own people did not accept him" (John 1:11), rejected by his disciples who at his betrayal and arrest all "deserted him and fled" (Matthew 26:56), rejected by religious leaders who falsely accused him of blasphemy, rejected by secular leaders who mocked him, beat him and nailed him to a cross. Jesus was "seen in a critical way." Jesus was "cut off, demeaned, isolated." Like David, Jesus was the rejected shepherd, the Good Shepherd who was rejected for you.

And on the cross, although rejected by nearly everyone, Jesus was not rejected by his Heavenly Father. In his cry of dereliction Jesus quoted the psalms—"My God, my God, why have you forsaken me?" (Psalm 22:1; Matthew 27:46; Mark 15:34). Jesus did *not* cry, "My Father, my Father, why have you forsaken me?" because his Heavenly Father was right there, gazing into his son's disfigured face, a face Jesus did not cover with an astronaut helmet or anything else, as God the Father said, "I love it. It's my son's face. I wanna see it." And this is why Luke records Jesus' final words as "Father, into your hands I commend my spirit" (Luke 23:46).

The gospel is good news for those have been rejected because on Good Friday Jesus was rejected for you. Moreover, scripture assures us that the Risen Jesus' words to those who have been rejected by others are "I will never leave you or forsake you" (Hebrews 13:5). In other words, even if you have been rejected and uninvited, the gospel means everyone will remain standing until you arrive and you will be anointed in the presence of those who have rejected you and filled mightily with the Spirit from that day forward because God has never rejected you.

On Good Friday Jesus was rejected for you, rejected in your place, because God would never and will never reject you. Since Jesus has been rejected for you, you have always been accepted by God, are now accepted by God, and will always be accepted by God—as we pray in the post-communion prayer every week, "Eternal God, Heavenly Father, you have graciously accepted us…" (*BCP* 365). And when you breathe your final earthly breath the same Heavenly Father into whose hands Jesus commended himself will be there to accept you and welcome you to your heavenly home, where you will be fully loved, fully accepted, world without end.

Amen.

All Will Be Made Alive in Christ

An Easter Sermon

If for this life only we have hoped in Christ, we are of all people most to be pitied. But in fact Christ has been raised from the dead, the first fruits of those who have died. For since death came through a human being, the resurrection of the dead has also come through a human being; for as all die in Adam, so all will be made alive in Christ (1 Corinthians 15:19-22).

In the Name of the Father, Son, and Holy Spirit.

Happy Easter! It is a joy to celebrate the resurrection of Jesus Christ with you today. On Easter we are reminded that Christianity is a resurrection faith, that death is not the end of the story for you because death was not the end of the story for Jesus Christ. Jesus indeed died, and Jesus was indeed raised from the dead.

Jesus did not come to earth just to be a good example, or to make you a better you, or to dispense *Reader's Digest* kinds of "Points to Ponder" or "Quotable Quotes," or to provide yet another religious entree in the food court of world religions. Jesus came to give life to the dead. He put it this way, "God so loved the world that he gave his only Son, so that everyone who believes in him may not perish but may have eternal life"; "I came that [you] may have life, and have it abundantly" (John 3:16; 10:10). Jesus came to do what only God can do: give life to the dead.

One of my favorite movies is the 1989 film *Dead Poets Society*, in which the late Robin Williams played an English professor at an exclusive boarding school. On the first day of class he leads his students to the glass-enclosed display of old team photos and trophies of students who had attended decades earlier. He tells them, "We are food for worms, lads. Believe it or not each and every one of us in this room is one day going to stop breathing, turn cold, and die." He continues:

> Peruse some of the faces from the past. You've walked past them many times but I don't think you've really looked at them. They're not that different from you, are they? Same haircuts, full of hormones, just like you—invincible, just like you feel. The world is their oyster. They believe they're destined for great things, just like many of you. Their eyes are full of hope, just like you. Did they wait until it was too late to make from their lives even one iota of what they were capable? Because, you see gentlemen, these boys are now fertilizing daffodils. But if you listen real close, you can hear them whisper their legacy to you. Go on, lean in. Listen, you hear it? "Carpe... carpe diem, seize the day, boys, make your lives extraordinary."

And he was right, our flesh is indeed destined to die, to feed worms, to fertilize daffodils. No matter how smart, wealthy, beautiful, talented, resourceful, hardworking, well-educated, well-connected, or witty you are, one day you will die. There is no way around it. It is an appointment you may be able to postpone but one you cannot cancel. One day the grim reaper will knock at your door. One day a bell marking your death will toll, and as the great priest and poet John Donne, wrote, "Never send to know for whom the bell tolls; it tolls for thee."

And so we may try to make our lives extraordinary. Along these lines you may have seen the motivational posters with a word or phrase and accompanying slogan to motivate us to do just that, posters like: "Excellence—Some excel because they are destined to, most excel because they are determined to" or "Potential—We all have the tools for greatness within us" or "Make It Happen—Some people want it to happen, some wish it would happen, others make it happen."

I actually prefer posters that poke fun at motivational posters, such as: "Teamwork—A few harmless flakes working together can unleash an avalanche of destruction" or "Consulting—If you're not a part of the solution, there's good money to be made in prolonging the problem" or "Believe in Yourself—Because the rest of us think you're an idiot" or my personal favorite: "Wishes—When you wish upon a falling star, your dreams can come true, unless it's really a meteor hurtling to earth which will destroy all life, then you're pretty much hosed no matter what you wish for, unless it's death by meteor."

And while there is nothing wrong with seizing the day and making your life extraordinary, and even if you like motivational posters, when it comes to death, it all falls short. The reality of death remains, as do the questions surrounding it. In what may be the most famous lines in all of English literature, Hamlet's "To be or not to be" soliloquy in Shakespeare's tragic masterpiece, the prince of Denmark reflects on the reality of his own mortality, his own future death:

> To die, to sleep;
> To sleep: perchance to dream: ay, there's the rub;
> For in that sleep of death what dreams may come
> When we have shuffled off this mortal coil,
> Must give us pause (*Hamlet* III.i.64-68).

Hamlet then describes his fear about after we "have shuffled off this mortal coil":

> The dread of something after death,
> The undiscover'd country from whose bourn
> No traveler returns (*Hamlet* III.i.78-80).

But on Easter we celebrate that Someone has actually returned from "the undiscovered country," Jesus Christ, the Son of God, who gives us real hope in the face of death. We need God to do what only God can do, give life to the dead. And that is exactly what God does through the death and resurrection of Jesus Christ, as we read in today's passage from Paul's First Letter to the Corinthians:

> If for this life only we have hoped in Christ, we are of all people most to be pitied. But in fact Christ has been raised from the dead, the first fruits of those who have died. For since death came through a human being, the resurrection of the dead has also come through a human being; for as all die in Adam, so all will be made alive in Christ (1 Corinthians 15:19-22).

"All will be made alive in Christ"—and that "all" includes you. Biblically resurrection is not so much about being reincarnated, or living on in the dreams and words of others, or playing a harp on a cloud. Biblically resurrection is about bodily resurrection, God transforming your dead body into a resurrected body. This gives us real hope in the midst of real suffering and real loss and real death.

In the Old Testament, the greatest example of this was Job, an admired man who in a very short time suffered the loss of his children, his wealth, and his health. As he mourned the loss of his children, as he sat in the ashes of his lost wealth that had all burned down, as he was covered from head to foot with sores from his lost health, his wife gave him the following advice, "Curse God, and die" (Job 2:9).

But Job would not do it. Even in the midst of his real suffering and the real loss of his children and the apparent imminence of his own real death, his hope in the bodily resurrection, his hope of God giving life to the dead, remained as he proclaimed, "I know that my Redeemer lives, and that at the last he will stand upon the earth; and after my skin has been destroyed, then in my flesh I shall see God, whom I shall see on my side, and my eyes shall behold, and not another" (Job 19:25-27). "In my flesh I shall see God," Job proclaimed. And you will too.

And in the New Testament scriptures assure us, "If the Spirit of him who raised Jesus from the dead dwells in you, he who raised Christ from the dead will give life to your mortal bodies also through his Spirit that dwells in you" (Romans 8:11)—that "the trumpet will sound, and the dead will be raised imperishable, and (you) will be changed" (1 Corinthians 15:52).

"All will be made alive in Christ..." This not only includes you, but also those whom you love who have died. Many years ago I was teaching a youth confirmation class and the kids were taking turns answering the question, "Who do want to see in heaven?" As you could imagine, their answers reflected their personalities and interests. One kid, a guitar enthusiast said, "I want to see Jimi Hendrix" and another, a political buff, said, "I want to see John F. Kennedy." One kid joked, "I want to see Ronald McDonald," which sparked a prolonged discussion about whether or not Ronald McDonald is real and if so, whether he is alive or dead—one of the joys of teaching a youth confirmation class.

But some of the kids answered from their heart: "I want to see my grandma and hear her read me stories again," "I want to see my brother and tell him I'm sorry," and "I want to see my dad again and give him a hug." On this Easter Sunday, how would you answer that question? Who do you want to see in heaven? You will, because Jesus Christ is risen, and "all will be made alive in Christ."

Two brief music illustrations, and then I will close... In 1964 legendary songwriter Curtis Mayfield wrote a song called "People Get Ready" that became a huge hit, a song Martin Luther King, Jr. named the unofficial anthem of the Civil Rights Movement, a song *Rolling Stone* magazine dubbed the twenty-fourth greatest song of all time, a song that compares salvation to being invited aboard a train:

> People get ready, there's a train a-comin'
> You don't need no baggage, you just get on board
> All you need is faith to hear the diesels hummin'
> You don't need no ticket, you just thank the Lord
> (The title track on The Impressions' 1965 album)

Several decades later Bruce Springsteen based his 1999 song, "Land of Hopes and Dreams" which has become a live concert show stopper, on Curtis Mayfield's song. Springsteen emphasized the universal hope of this train of salvation:

> This train carries saints and sinners
> This train carries losers and winners
> This train carries whores and gamblers
> This train carries lost souls
> This train carries broken hearted
> This train thieves and sweet souls departed
> This train carries fools and kings
> This train, all aboard
> (On his 2001 album *Live in New York City*)

And the good news of the gospel is that this train also carries you.

And you probably guessed the identity of the Engineer of this salvation train, Jesus Christ, who died for you and was raised for you. No matter how extraordinary or ordinary your life is, the final word belongs to the One whose love for you has always been extraordinary.

This means when your appointment with death arrives you will not be alone in the waiting room, that when the grim reaper knocks on your door, that knock will be dwarfed by Someone Else knocking on your door, that the bell that will toll at your death will be the bell that tolls at the beginning of your eternal life, that your death will not the end of your story but rather what C. S. Lewis called "Chapter One of the Great Story, which no one on earth has read: which goes on forever: in which every chapter is better than the one before" (*The Last Battle* 228).

Jesus Christ is risen, and he will do what only God can do, give life to the dead.

All will be made alive in Christ, including you.

You don't need no ticket. You just thank the Lord.

Amen.

Made in the USA
Columbia, SC
10 January 2023